Unhurried

Devotions & Prayers
for Savoring
Quiet Time with God

Print ISBN 978-1-68322-599-7

eBook Editions:
Adobe Digital Edition (.epub) 978-1-68322-574-4
Kindle and MobiPocket Edition (prc.) 978-1-68322-573-7

Published by Barbour Books, an imprint of Barbour Publishing, Inc., 1810 Barbour Drive, Uhrichsville, Ohio 44683, www.barbourbooks.com.

Our mission is to inspire the world with the life-changing message of the Bible.

Member of the
Evangelical Christian
Publishers Association

Printed in China.

Unhurried

Devotions & Prayers
for Savoring
Quiet Time with God

Jessie Fioritto

BARBOUR BOOKS
An Imprint of Barbour Publishing, Inc.

Introduction

Are you exhausted by the crush of life? Do you question whether there is real meaning behind all this activity?

Take a moment to breathe. Step out from under the pressure to accumulate and to perform, and enter into the abundant life God meant you to live. Your life may not look like what you imagined, or even what you thought you wanted. So pause in the middle of your hectic rat race and ask for the good way. Trek down ancient paths hand in hand with your Creator. Not only will you find rest for your careworn soul, but He will take you deeper than you ever thought you could go and teach you what you didn't know you needed to learn.

Choosing this road brings trials. You'll be tested, and you'll learn to abandon yourself to Jesus. He doesn't offer a spa-day life, but falling for Jesus is the adventure you've longed for. And the journey promises fulfillment, soul rest, and eternal reward—an incorruptible crown. So surrender your life of burnout and frazzled nerves. Slow the chase for self-fulfilling desires, and simply abide in Jesus. Invite Him to change the way you think.

Unhurried doesn't have to mean "unbusy." Remember that someone who always made time for you? Be that person with God. Open yourself to His spectacular, one-of-a-kind plan for you.

Fall for Him

*And in the morning, rising up a great
while before day, he went out, and departed
into a solitary place, and there prayed.*
MARK 1:35

Early morning—when the day is pregnant with possibility. The sun has yet to lift her face fully above the horizon, the grass weeps in joy for the new day, and the birds cheer its coming. Genesis says that God walked in the garden of Eden "in the cool of the day" (3:8). Maybe it was morning. It's reminiscent of the scene in *Pride and Prejudice* where Elizabeth rises early and walks in the dim, predawn mist. She looks up as Darcy strides purposefully toward her through the dew-laden grass. She waits for him. And he meets her, pressing his forehead to hers as the sun breaks the plane where heaven touches earth, transfiguring them in golden radiance. You, too, can relish the practice of welcoming the day in the embrace of the lover of your soul.

Many of God's servants abandoned their beds to meet with Him in the early hours of the day. Abraham got up "early in the morning to the place where he stood before the LORD" (Genesis 19:27). Scripture records that Moses, Joshua, Hannah, Samuel, David, Job, Mary, and the apostles all rose early to fellowship and deal in the business of God. (See Exodus 24:4; Joshua 6:12; 1 Samuel 1:19; 15:12; 17:20; Job 1:5; Luke 24:22; Acts 5:21.) Jesus also rose early to pray and often sought solitary places to be alone with His Father.

But there's a reason so many of us brandish coffee mugs

6

that warn "I don't do mornings." So what mysterious draw compelled these men and women to forfeit warmth and sleep to seek God? With the example of our Lord and so many heroes of faith before us, why do we too often fail to pull ourselves from the comfort of our beds for a few quiet moments with God?

The answer lies in relationship. It's difficult to be motivated by the cold promise of a checklist when compared to the warm embrace of a loved one. Elizabeth awaited her only love as the fog hung low over the fields. Quiet time isn't about studying a book. Jesus delights in us and can't get enough of our presence. He is waiting to soothe us and sing to us in joy (Zephaniah 3:17). Sounds a lot like falling in love, doesn't it? So rise up early in the morning. Find a secret place and fall madly in love with Jesus.

Jesus, lover of my soul, my friend.
Meet me early. I want to be with You, worship You,
and go away marked by Your glory. Amen.

Prince of Peace

These things I have spoken unto you, that in me ye might have peace. In the world ye shall have tribulation: but be of good cheer; I have overcome the world.
JOHN 16:33

Have you ever engaged in a little Dumpster diving on trash day? Come on, admit it. Perhaps you found a discarded gem left by the roadside for the taking—an antique piece of furniture with great potential or an old bike. You saw its value and snatched it up.

Peace of mind—although it holds incomparable worth, no currency can purchase it. We amass fortunes, yet our bodies are bankrupted by incurable diseases, our minds impoverished by anxiety. Like an original Da Vinci orphaned on the garbage-day curb, the sacred ground of our inner being is often left unprotected—unguarded and vulnerable. Our fragile state of mind is strafed by the enemy fire of outside circumstances while our own Judas thoughts engage in the demoralizing saturation bombing of negative self-talk.

Friend, what if you discovered that while invaluable, peace has been freely extended to you on the palm of a nail-scarred hand? This priceless commodity is actually being given away. It rests alongside the fast-flowing freeway of the world, waiting for someone to see it for the treasure it is and take it up for themselves. Jesus said, "Peace I leave with you, my peace I give unto you: not as the world giveth, give I unto you. Let not your heart be troubled, neither let it be afraid" (John 14:27).

But how can this promise of untroubled tranquility of the mind possibly be fulfilled in such an evil and uncertain world? To find the answer, you have to look beyond this speck of time. You have to cast your vision into eternity. Our state of peace springs from the fountain of God's mercy. It flows from our reconciliation with God through Christ's death. He took our whipping on His own back, and God's justice no longer condemns us to death. Jesus restored our relationship with the living God—our eternal soul is saved! And this abbreviated life is but a prologue to eternity—to our real life—forever with Him. When we gain heavenly foresight, the sentinel of God's peace is set over us: "The peace of God, which passeth all understanding, shall keep your hearts and minds through Christ Jesus" (Philippians 4:7). God's peace is the watchdog our minds need to truly rest in spite of our circumstances.

Heavenly Father, set Your peace as a guard at the perimeter of my mind and heart. Keep my hope focused beyond this place of trouble and sin to the future I will have with You. It is both beautiful and good. There I will truly experience Your perfect peace. Amen.

The King's Daughter

*I will receive you. And will be a Father
unto you, and ye shall be my sons and
daughters, saith the Lord Almighty.*
2 CORINTHIANS 6:17–18

Pink glitter dances in the light as dress-up shoes clomp across the floor on the feet of a tiny, dimpled girl arrayed in a flounced tulle skirt and Hello Kitty sunglasses. She slings the tail of her hot-pink feather boa over her shoulder with a dainty hand encased in white evening gloves that pile in folds up her forearms. Her untamed hair is crowned with a bejeweled tiara. "Look, Mommy, I'm a princess!"

Little girls love to dream about the fairy-tale life of sparkling princesses. But once we've grown, we put aside fables and daydreams of ball gowns, royalty, and shining white knights—well, most of us put away our feather boas and Hello Kitty sunglasses, anyway! And in truth we don't have to tuck away all of our visions in cedar-lined wardrobes.

You are a daughter of the King. The High King of heaven is your Father. And while you may have to forfeit that tiara in this world, your Father above will adorn you in the priceless jewels of virtue (Proverbs 31:10), the finest robes of white (Revelation 3:5), and eternal crowns—the imperishable crown (1 Corinthians 9:25), the crown of life (James 1:12), the crown of righteousness (2 Timothy 4:8), the crown of rejoicing (1 Thessalonians 2:19), and the crown of glory (1 Peter 5:4).

"For those who are led by the Spirit of God are the children of God. The Spirit you received does not make you slaves, so that you live in fear again; rather, the Spirit you received brought about your adoption to sonship. And by him we cry, '*Abba*, Father.' The Spirit himself testifies with our spirit that we are God's children. Now if we are children, then we are heirs—heirs of God and co-heirs with Christ, if indeed we share in his sufferings in order that we may also share in his glory" (Romans 8:14–17 NIV).

Whether your love for your earthly father is as full as the belled skirt of a ball gown or as limp as yesterday's T-shirt, whether you feel you've been held dear or abandoned by him, daughter, your faith in Jesus is the seal on your adoption papers. You are now the King's beloved child! You are cherished. You are protected. You are His heir with Christ, and your inheritance awaits in eternity. Someday the gossamer veil of this world will be lifted, and you will take your place at your Father's table—at the King's feast!

God, You are truly my Father! And I am Your child, the apple of Your eye. Teach me to walk in virtue as is fitting for the King's daughter. I know that You will never remove Your guiding hand from my life. Amen.

Win Your Crown

*The four and twenty elders fall down before him
that sat on the throne, and worship him that liveth
for ever and ever, and cast their crowns before
the throne, saying, Thou art worthy, O Lord.*
REVELATION 4:10–11

You dredge up the final remnant of energy from your exhausted body, driving well beyond the limit of your reserve when you glimpse the finish line. With every cell in your being, you strain forward on fatigued legs. Through the weary eyes of your depleted strength, even the flimsy tape across the finish seems fortified with concrete. In a beat of your hammering heart, every agonizing moment of training flits through your mind as your spent body breaks the plane of the ribbon. You've won the race! You've finished well. Rib cage heaving, you bend over to breathe in the glory of the prize.

Paul must have known a thing or two about physical training. You get the feeling he has fought the internal war between a wasted body that wants to surrender and a will that presses on in spite of it to win the race. He tells the Corinthian church: "Know ye not that they which run in a race run all, but one receiveth the prize? So run, that ye may obtain. And every man that striveth for the mastery is temperate in all things. Now they do it to obtain a corruptible crown; but we an incorruptible" (1 Corinthians 9:24–25). This Christian race requires training and endurance. The Corinthian athletes were running for a perishable wreath. But our prize is an eternal crown of glory (1 Peter 5:4).

Paul goes on to say, "I therefore so run, not as uncertainly; so fight I, not as one that beateth the air: but I keep under my body, and bring it into subjection: lest that by any means, when I have preached to others, I myself should be a castaway" (1 Corinthians 9:26–27). Let's not deceive ourselves. Training is hard. The New International Version translates verse 27 as "I strike a blow to my body and make it my slave." Surely Paul must have experienced the day after a workout—that next morning when long-dormant muscles scream their existence as if your pillow took a tire iron to them while you slept.

Training spiritually to resist sin is no different. Sometimes we want to give in and eat that ice cream of immorality. A little gossip here, a white lie there, or maybe you've caved to sexual sin or pride—dig out those training shoes of God's Word and bring your body into subjection. Make it your slave! Master your urges like a marathon runner in training so you will win your crown in glory.

Father God, make me the master over sin that tempts me to forfeit the race. You alone are worthy! Amen.

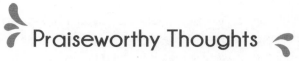

Praiseworthy Thoughts

*The heavens declare the glory of God; and the
firmament sheweth his handywork. . . . Let the words of
my mouth, and the meditation of my heart, be acceptable
in thy sight, O LORD, my strength, and my redeemer.*
PSALM 19:1, 14

Does your mind ever get a bad attitude? Why is it that your thoughts will skip, laughing hand in hand with hopelessness, down the rutted road of negativity and right into the graveyard of depression and discontent? And before you know it, you've thrown down your welcome mat in the tumbledown shack of unhappiness. You swat some cobwebs and plug in your Keurig for company—only to realize that your friends have fled your gloomy abode as if you were dishing up last week's brussels sprouts.

Yes, we've all slinked away from conversations feeling like the thundercloud that broke over the Fourth of July picnic, scattering everyone for cover and erasing the sun from their sky—no one wants to invite all *that* to the party. But you don't have to be that person. You don't have to entertain such destructive thoughts. You can choose the topic of your brain's endless blog posts. You can be the moderator of your inner monologue. In fact, you should be!

Don't let negative thoughts and attitudes tie you in knots like unruly kids left too long without correction. Go Mary Poppins on their bad mood! Take them in hand. Discipline your mind to search out the good around you. Find the spoonful of sugar that's missing from your method of living. And be aware of the landscape of your mind. If you realize you've gotten on the wrong train of thought, get off that train, sister! Buy yourself a new ticket and "be renewed in the spirit of your mind. . .that ye put on the new man, which after God is created in righteousness and true holiness" (Ephesians 4:23–24).

Dragging your mind out of its old way of thinking can feel like pushing a boulder up Everest, so here's Paul's advice for emptying the garbage can of your mind: "Whatsoever things are true, whatsoever things are honest, whatsoever things are just, whatsoever things are pure, whatsoever things are lovely, whatsoever things are of good report; if there be any virtue, and if there be any praise, think on these things" (Philippians 4:8).

Where do your thoughts linger? Today, let those old negative musings die of neglect in that abandoned shack, and instead, find something true, pure, lovely, or praiseworthy and think about that.

God, alert me when my thoughts run wildly toward criticism, judgment, and complaints. Teach me to corral my thoughts within Your parameters of encouragement and purity. Amen.

Your Father's Heart

He delighteth in mercy. . .he will have
compassion upon us. . .and thou wilt cast
all their sins into the depths of the sea.
MICAH 7:18–19

Have you ever wondered if God cares? Does He seem distant to you? This world is full of violence, evil, and chaos. Why? Does God see any of us?

My friend, Jesus doesn't want you to battle these questions without answer. So He showed you the Father's heart through story.

A younger son demanded his inheritance from his father. So the father gave it to him, and the son left home and blew everything he'd received on wild living. Then hard times (or perhaps divine discipline) hit. Famine swept the country, so the son hired himself out to slop pigs. While his mouth was watering over the pig slop, he came to his senses. *What am I doing here?* he thought. *My father's servants eat better than this! And I'm starving to death here with the pigs.* So in humiliation (it's hard to have pride with pig slop on your face) he went back to beg his father to hire him as a servant.

His father saw him coming home a long way off. And he was moved with compassion for him. Have you ever encountered someone in such a gut-wrenching situation that you were viscerally crushed with compassion for their plight? Have you ever seen pictures of starving orphans? That's the emotion this father experienced at the sight of his starving, broken, wayward son. The Greek word here means "to have the bowels yearn, to pity, to be moved with compassion."* The father saw the son, and his gut clenched with his aching need to hold him in his arms again, just as he had when he was an innocent child—to wipe his tears and comfort him.

And the father ran out to meet his son, forgetting propriety and everything else except that his boy was back. He threw his arms around him and kissed him. Can you just imagine the father cupping his son's head to his shoulder and rocking gently, tears of joy stinging his eyes?

The son cried out, "Father, I have sinned against heaven and you! I'm not worthy to be called your son." But the father shushed his protests. "Quick," he told his servants. "I need the best robe, a ring for his finger, and sandals! Bring the fatted calf! We're going to celebrate! For my son was dead and is alive again; he was lost and is found!" (see Luke 15:11–24).

Beloved, this father is also your Father. If you have sinned, return to Him. He longs for you, waits for you. He loves you.

*Father, my heart overflows with sorrow for my
sin that has caused You grief. Forgive me. Amen.*

*Strong's Definitions, s.v. "splagchnizomai," *Blue Letter Bible*, https://www.blueletterbible.org/lang/lexicon/lexicon.cfm?Strongs=G4697&t=KJV.

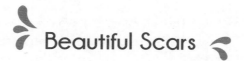

Beautiful Scars

*We glory in tribulations also: knowing that
tribulation worketh patience; and patience,
experience; and experience, hope: and hope
maketh not ashamed; because the love of
God is shed abroad in our hearts by the
Holy Ghost which is given unto us.*
ROMANS 5:3–5

People drive from all around to stay at an old grain mill that was converted to an inn, to soak in the history and unplug for a while. The rough wood planks are exposed on almost every wall, and the ancient hardwood floors, patched and worn, are scarred with a century of stories. The walls are pocked with nail holes, and water stains bleed down their sides. But the markings only add to the depth and character of its grain. It is breathtakingly beautiful.

This wood has been tempered by its life. Have you ever tried to drive a nail into century-old oak? It's like beating on granite. Aged wood possesses both beauty and strength.

We've all been scuffed up by life. Sometimes it feels as if the cold blade of fate has carved deep grooves in your soul. The pain cuts. It threatens to break you and leave you in a dark and hopeless grave. Your bruised life doesn't make sense, and your mind recoils at the injustice and senselessness. You ask "Why?" a thousand times but never get a satisfying answer. You feel haggard, ugly, beaten.

When hard things come into your life, look for God's path

through it, for the opportunity to grow and deepen your faith. We have two choices in the midst of trial and pain. We can either allow our hardships to drive us away from God or propel us toward Him. We can become bitter and angry at our circumstances, or we can trust God to finish the good work He started in us (Philippians 1:6).

The apostle Paul said that we should glory in our suffering because of its benefits. Glorying in your suffering releases a cascade of blessing from God to counteract Satan's schemes to crush you and bind you in darkness, because suffering leads to patient endurance, and endurance develops your character, and strong character will strengthen your confident hope of salvation (Romans 5:3–5). So grab ahold of this hope in the hard times. You won't be disappointed by it.

Satan intends to break us. He must be very frustrated when God continues to work His love and goodness into our lives through the pain. Friend, with God you can do hard things beautifully.

God, take my scarred-up life and redeem its beauty for Your purpose. Through my trials You can teach me patience and character. And I will not be disappointed by my hope in Your salvation! In Jesus' powerful name, amen.

135,000 Foes

*My grace is sufficient for thee: for my
strength is made perfect in weakness.*
2 Corinthians 12:9

Gideon was hiding in a hole. Determined to thresh his wheat despite the threat of Israel's oppressive enemy, the Midianites, who were destroying Israel's crops and killing their herds, Gideon took cover in an old winepress—a stone pit where grapes were crushed to squeeze out the juice. Israel was in a dark time. They had wandered and worshipped false gods. When they cried out for God to save them, the angel of the Lord, a preincarnate manifestation of Christ, sought out Gideon.

"The Lord is with thee, thou mighty man of valour" (Judges 6:12). Can't you just imagine Gideon's swift glance over his shoulder? *Who? Me?* His thoughts had to be tracking somewhere along the lines of *God, You're betting on the wrong horse here.* But "God resisteth the proud, and giveth grace to the humble" (1 Peter 5:5). Gideon showed his humble spirit by admitting that he was from the weakest clan and the least in his family. Proud he was not. But he was a willing and obedient servant of the Lord. And instead of addressing him according to his circumstances, God named him what He would make of him—mighty warrior.

What follows could have been ripped from the story line of the next Marvel movie—impossible odds, cruel villains, and an underdog. Iron Man and Thor, step aside. God tells Gideon to gather the troops. But He isn't satisfied with the thirty-two thousand men Gideon amassed. "No, no, you have too many men, Gideon. Send the scared ones home." Gideon's eyebrows must have shot up when his number was slashed to ten thousand. "Hmm," God says. "Still too risky. Thin the ranks a little more." To Gideon's probable horror, three hundred men remain. "Better." God nods in satisfaction. "Now the odds are so ridiculous that everyone will know for sure that this is My victory." The Midianite army numbered 135,000.

In the end, 120,000 enemy swordsmen lay dead on the battlefield. God's power is always enough! Take heart when the odds are stacked against you, friend. God may be about to flex His muscles on your behalf. If God has asked you to do something outside your own strength—whether that means being patient with your children, teaching Sunday school, or building a world-changing organization—God needs only your willingness and obedience to accomplish the impossible!

*God, bring me to a place of trust in You
so steadfast that I can live radically beyond
my ability. I'm so thankful that with You I can
accomplish anything You ask of me because You
are with me. In Jesus' powerful name, amen.*

Collateral Beauty

*The LORD is nigh unto them
that are of a broken heart.*
PSALM 34:18

A mother grieves in a hospital hallway. Her six-year-old daughter is about to be taken off life support. The woman sitting beside her asks who she is losing. And then the woman offers a piece of advice: "Don't forget to look for the collateral beauty." In the moment of our suffering, beauty out of pain, life out of ashes offends us. Personal growth is a cold substitute for our loss. All we feel is aching want for the piece of our broken life that's now missing. But, precious, hurting sister, God is at work.

A father's mourning is so deep that, like Job, he sits in silence—unable to work, unable to eat, unable to utter the name of the child he's lost. He offered up his life for hers, but it was rejected. And the pain has shattered his joy into a thousand shards that pierce him.

This is the scenario that plays out in the film *Collateral Beauty*. Howard has lost his daughter, and now his despondency is threatening the livelihood of his ad agency partners. His friends, in a misguided attempt to bring him back and save their company, hire actors to convince him he's being visited by Death, Time, and Love to prove his mental instability and seize his company shares. Howard has a strikingly Christlike moment when he sits in a conference room with his partners, Whit, Claire, and Simon.

His friends have been his Judas. But in the face of their

betrayal, he responds to them with deep love. He assures Simon that he knows he's dying and that he will provide for his family. He encourages Claire not to give up on having a child and says he's proud of her and her personal sacrifice for the company. He tells Whit he's the best friend he's ever had, but he needs to win back his daughter's love. And then he signs over his shares.

Pain can wield a harsh chisel. It will carve you, and it's up to you what you're formed into. You can become the shavings of anger and bitterness, or you can become the sculpture, an ordinary block made beautiful through loss.

Allow your pain to sensitize you to the pain of others so you can love them better. Love's words to Howard ring true of God: "I am the only 'why.'. . . I was there in her laugh, but I am also here now in your pain. Do not try to live without me."*

God, I hurt. But You are here with me. Help me look to my pain for a hint of Your plan in my life. Show me its worth in opening my eyes to a hurting world. Amen.

Collateral Beauty, directed by David Frankel (Warner Bros., 2016), DVD.

Giant Slayer

The thunder of his power who can understand?
JOB 26:14

The Israelites were shaking in their sandals. The Philistine army had aligned against them across the valley. Their arrogant champion, standing over nine feet tall, sported heavy bronze armor. Goliath paced the battle line, daring any of Saul's soldiers to scrape up some nerve and fight him. But the Israelites' terror of Goliath betrayed their waning faith in the almighty God. They had abandoned God as their king and demanded a human ruler on the throne of Israel, and now they had also forgotten their faith in God's covenant promises to vanquish their enemies. That is, until a young boy with guts and faith bigger than a roaring giant stepped to the front with a sling and five rocks—backed by the mighty hand of his awesome God.

It's important to note that David's faith in God's ability to defeat Goliath didn't just spring into existence spontaneously when he heard the giant's mocking catcalls. He didn't run out to challenge Goliath with no prior experience. David had history with God, even as a young boy. He was a shepherd, a dangerous occupation in those days. God had helped him protect his lambs from dangerous predators and had taught David to trust in His strength in the wilderness, much as He had the Israelites when He delivered them from Egypt.

So when no one would challenge Goliath, David told King Saul, "Thy servant slew both the lion and the bear: and this uncircumcised Philistine shall be as one of them, seeing he hath defied the armies of the living God" (1 Samuel 17:36). Fueled by faith that God would fight for him, David went forward to meet the giant. And most likely met uproarious laughter from the enemy. Goliath ridiculed David: "Am I a dog, that you come at me with sticks?" (1 Samuel 17:43 NIV). But David was not cowed. "Thou comest to me with a sword, and with a spear, and with a shield: but I come to thee in the name of the LORD of hosts, the God of the armies of Israel, whom thou hast defied" (1 Samuel 17:45). David ran toward the battle line and released a single stone from his sling. The giant collapsed facedown, David's rock embedded in his forehead.

Instead of sizing up the problem, David focused on the all-powerful God he served and His promises. His story inspires as we watch a young boy place utter faith in God's might to kill a giant. And we want to slay giants in our own lives. Friend, if you're facing enormous problems, don't tremble at their size. Place your trust in the Lord of hosts who is mighty to save.

Lord of heaven's armies, You are the all-powerful God of the universe. Give me faith never to underestimate Your capabilities. Amen.

Grace

And the Word was made flesh, and dwelt among us,
(and we beheld his glory, the glory as of the only
begotten of the Father), full of grace and truth.

JOHN 1:14

Her head hung low in shame as she was dragged down the dusty street. The morning sun glared at her from atop the horizon, its accusing stare matching that of everyone she passed. Her cheeks blazed as crimson as the awakening sky, and she trembled at the realization that today could be her last. Her transgression carried the penalty of death.

The Pharisees pushed her to the front of the crowd gathered at the temple. The teacher named Jesus was speaking to the people. She refused to look at Him or anyone else as the Pharisees uncovered her shame for all to see: "Master, this woman was taken in adultery, in the very act. Now Moses in the law commanded us, that such should be stoned: but what sayest thou?" (John 8:4–5).

A blanket of stillness smothered the crowd's murmuring. What would Jesus say about her sin? She waited for Him to condemn her. The silence stretched painfully, and she glanced at Jesus. What on earth was He doing? Instead of answering the crowd, He was scribbling in the dirt. Was He crazy?

The Pharisees demanded an answer until finally Jesus stood. "He that is without sin among you, let him first cast a stone at her," He said. Then He knelt down to write in the dust again. She couldn't believe it! One by one her accusers

26

shuffled away until she stood alone with Jesus. His gentle eyes met her tear-reddened ones. "Where are your accusers?" He asked. "Didn't even one of them condemn you?"

"No, Lord," she whispered.

His mouth tipped in a smile. "Neither do I. Go and sin no more."

Incredible! Jesus, the One she'd heard was the Messiah, hadn't condemned her. He hadn't deemed her worthless because of her sin!

Grace. It's shocking. It's love without conditions. Jesus, the Holy One, the One entrusted with all judgment (John 5:22) didn't throw stones at this woman. He didn't condemn her for what she'd done. He didn't throw her life away because of the sin she'd committed. Instead, He said, "I came to free you. Go. Live free from sin and condemnation."

Jesus came to deliver you from your sin, beloved, not condemn you because of it. Your life is precious to Him because of who you are—a chosen daughter—not because of what you do. Go and sin no more.

❧

Jesus, I thought You would be angry about what I've done. I thought I would see judgment in Your eyes. But instead, I encountered the liberating power of grace. Thank You, Jesus! My shame has dissolved in the cleansing wash of Your love. Amen.

Words of Life

Do not let any unwholesome talk come out of your mouths,
but only what is helpful for building others up according
to their needs, that it may benefit those who listen.
EPHESIANS 4:29 NIV

Are your words helpful? It's a good standard to consider. If we don't pause and hear what we're saying, we might miss the destruction left behind in the wake of our motor mouths. Are we constantly complaining, criticizing, or gossiping? Or do our words encourage? Do people feel better or worse after a conversation with us?

Joshua was poised to succeed Moses and lead the Israelites into the promised land without his mentor. He must have been nervous about his ability to fill the sandals of the great prophet, the friend of God who talked to Him face-to-face. The Israelites had wandered the arid desert for forty years. Joshua surely was determined to possess the land—to finally have a home.

But he'd stepped into the role of leading a downtrodden people. A young commander with a dying teacher, facing a war to inhabit new lands, Joshua must have craved encouragement. His confidence and faith could have been flung from their soaring heights and shattered on the jagged rocks of doubtful or critical words from his mentor.

But Moses knew how to coax life and hope into glorious blossom with his words. "Be strong and of a good courage: for thou must go with this people unto the land which the LORD hath sworn unto their fathers to give them; and thou shalt cause them to inherit it. And the LORD, he it is that doth go before thee; he will be with thee, he will not fail thee, neither forsake thee: fear not, neither be dismayed" (Deuteronomy 31:7–8).

Moses continued to uplift Joshua with the truth of God's promises. Joshua is encouraged to "be strong and courageous" seven times before they cross the Jordan River. God Himself bolstered Joshua: "Be strong and of a good courage: for thou shalt bring the children of Israel into the land which I sware unto them: and I will be with thee" (Deuteronomy 31:23).

Words have power—both the authority to command us into hope and sentence us to despair. Proverbs 15:4 (NIV) says, "The soothing tongue is a tree of life, but a perverse tongue crushes the spirit." Do you speak life? Do you know how? Or have you settled into the habit of complaining and criticizing everything and everyone? It's horrifyingly easy to desolate others with words, but with a little self-control and effort, you can begin to uplift—you can become a tree of life instead of a bleak skeletal twig.

Heavenly Father, guard my tongue. Teach me to encourage others and speak life instead of crushing spirits with harsh words. Amen.

Experts in Goodness

For the wisdom of this world is foolishness in God's sight.
As it is written: "He catches the wise in their craftiness."
1 CORINTHIANS 3:19 NIV

Childhood. Sunny summers of fun and freedom. Friends, carefree happiness, a future spread like a delicious picnic of possibility before us. Somehow the happy and good moments seem amplified by the filter of our nostalgic remembrances, as if our hope-filled childlike perspective is resurrected by our memories. We sometimes joke about the appeal of living forever in childhood. But our rose-colored lens can also cast the truth of our adolescence in the enchanting stage lighting of fond memories. The emotional turbulence, the confusion, the near-sighted perspective of youth that often got us into trouble take on a rosy glow. We brush aside the injuries inflicted by the honed edge of our past inexperience. As much as we fondly remember it, childhood is not a destination but a highway to maturity.

Paul also encouraged believers not to linger in spiritual childhood. "Brethren, be not children in understanding: howbeit in malice be ye children, but in understanding be men" (1 Corinthians 14:20). The Greek word for *understanding* in this verse "refers to the ability not just to think, but also to control one's thoughts and attitudes."* He's saying grow up in your spirituality—learn some control!

Again in Romans 16:19 Paul wrote, "I would have you wise unto that which is good, and simple concerning evil." We spend years being educated, but how much time do we dedicate to understanding God's ways?

But wisdom also means skillfully applying what we've learned. Head knowledge about landing an airplane is useless if we can't translate it to the controls in front of us and safely touch down. And neither will a brain full of theology do us a bit of good if we don't live it.

This idea of excellence in goodness and inexperience in evil actually came from Jesus, who said, "Be ye therefore wise as serpents, and harmless as doves" (Matthew 10:16). But don't be confused. Being harmless as a dove doesn't equal naiveté. It really refers to your own motives and purity—a total rejection of evil in your thoughts and actions.[†] In Philippians Paul gives an example of how this looks: "Do all things without murmurings and disputings: that ye may be blameless and harmless, the sons of God, without rebuke, in the midst of a crooked and perverse nation, among whom ye shine as lights in the world; holding forth the word of life" (Philippians 2:14–16).

Do you shine as a blameless and harmless light? Graduate to the level of expert in goodness.

Jesus, I want to be excellent at what is good and innocent of all forms of evil. Purify my thoughts and actions from evil. Amen.

---

*Spiros Zodhiates, ed., "New Testament Lexical Aids," *Hebrew-Greek Keyword Study Bible* (Chattanooga, TN: AMG, 1996), 1684.
†Ibid., 1581.

To Know and Be Known

Be still, and know that I am God: I will be exalted among the heathen, I will be exalted in the earth.
PSALM 46:10

God longs to have a relationship with you. How amazing is that? The God of the universe wants to know you and be known by you. He is the Potter who formed you, inside and out. He knows you more intimately than any other, and His Son, Jesus, died for you. Because of Jesus, we can experience God in close relationship as Adam and Eve did when they strolled garden paths side by side with their Creator.

But this shall be the covenant that I will make with the house of Israel; After those days, saith the LORD, I will put my law in their inward parts, and write it in their hearts; and will be their God, and they shall be my people. And they shall teach no more every man his neighbour, and every man his brother, saying, Know the LORD: for they shall all know me, from the least of them unto the greatest of them, saith the LORD: for I will forgive their iniquity, and I will remember their sin no more. (Jeremiah 31:33–34)

Sometimes we can't get close to certain people. We try to be a friend and understand, but they don't reciprocate. But God says He wants a relationship with all people, "from the least of them unto the greatest of them." He wants to be known by all of us—by you. Regardless of your status, the God of love won't refuse to show Himself to you. "And ye shall seek me, and find me, when ye shall search for me with all your heart" (Jeremiah 29:13).

God's greatest desire is for you to know Him, but He also doesn't force Himself on anyone. If you go looking for Him, you will encounter the living God. If you are willing, He wants to do life with you. He wants you to experience Him in relationship by walking through life together just as you do with your loved ones now. Each shared experience takes your relationship deeper.

God invites us to taste and see that He is good (Psalm 34:8). When we seek God, we will experience His marvelous attributes as we come to know Him more—we discover His love (Ephesians 3:19), learn to recognize His voice (John 10:27), join in His plans both for us and the world (1 Peter 2:9), gain His freedom (Galatians 5:1), experience His peace (John 14:27), and find His rest for our souls (Matthew 11:28–30).

Seek to make knowing God the driving purpose of your life. He loves you and paid the ultimate price to have a relationship with you.

*Father God, show me more of You. I want to
see Your face and experience You. Amen.*

Mirror, Mirror

For all have sinned, and come
short of the glory of God.
ROMANS 3:23

Have you ever been ashamed of yourself—engaged in cringe-worthy behavior that left you echoing Tom Hanks's character in *You've Got Mail*? "Do you ever feel you've become the worst version of yourself? That a Pandora's box of all the secret, hateful parts—your arrogance, your spite, your condescension—has sprung open? Someone upsets you and instead of smiling and moving on, you zing them. 'Hello, it's Mr. Nasty.'"*

We've all lived this moment. The question is what do we do when confronted with our own capacity for sin? The book of James says that if we hear God's Word but don't do what it says, we're like a man who stares into a mirror and then walks away and forgets what he looks like (James 1:23–24).

Scripture has the unique power to show us who we really are. A brave pastor once admitted to his congregation during a sermon that as a young man he'd thumbed twenty dollars out of the offering plate one Sunday. A few gasps punctuated the silence. "I know what you're thinking!" he said. "You're a bad person!"

And it's true. But so are we all. We're all capable of being our worst self. But too often pride blinds us as we mount our hypercritical high horse like the Pharisee in Luke 18: "Thank You, God, that I am not like other people—cheaters, sinners, adulterers. I'm certainly not like that tax collector!"

34

God calls us to walk humbly with Him (Micah 6:8). And humility means seeing ourselves as we truly are. While the Pharisee preened in arrogance, the tax collector "standing afar off, would not lift up so much as his eyes unto heaven, but smote upon his breast, saying, God be merciful to me a sinner" (Luke 18:13). We will never stop judging others for their failures until we can own our bad behavior, poor choices, and self-serving motives and admit that we're wretched sinners.

If we see ourselves honestly through the looking glass of scripture, we will be empowered to deal in grace instead of judgment. "For by grace are ye saved through faith; and that not of yourselves: it is the gift of God: not of works, lest any man should boast" (Ephesians 2:8–9). When we experience the amazing grace God has treated us to in spite of our horrific ability to sin, grace will spill over into all of our interactions.

Heavenly Father, I am a sinner unworthy of mercy from a holy God. But You've gifted me with grace I could never afford. Show me how to love justice and mercy and walk humbly with You. In Jesus' name, amen.

You've Got Mail, directed by Nora Ephron (Warner Bros., 1998), DVD.

Restored

*Having forgiven you all trespasses. . .and took
[them] out of the way, nailing [them] to his cross.*
COLOSSIANS 2:13–14

"Lord, why can't I go with You now? I will lay down my life for
You!" Jesus was leaving them. And in his typical all-or-nothing
style, Peter committed to the ultimate sacrifice to stay with Jesus.
"Will you really, Peter?" Jesus' eyes must have been brimming
with knowing pain as He told Peter of his three pending denials.
"Simon, Simon," Jesus warned him, "Satan has asked to sift
you like wheat. But I have prayed for you, Simon, that your faith
may not fail. And when you have turned back, strengthen your
brothers." Hear the compassion and encouragement in Jesus'
tone—not *if* you turn back, but *when*, Peter.

Later that night, the disciples followed Jesus to the Mount
of Olives. Peter's night of terror began in earnest with the slash
of his sword. But Jesus went willingly with His captors, and
Peter and the others fled the scene of His arrest.

Peter and presumably John followed the mob at a distance.
They gained entrance to the high priest's courtyard and warmed
themselves by the fire, likely shivering from more than cold.
Peter had denied knowing Jesus twice. And then someone
asked, "Didn't I see you earlier in the olive grove with Jesus?"
Heart hammering on adrenaline, Peter shouted, "I don't know
what you're talking about!"

A rooster crowed in the pale dawn. Jesus turned and stared
straight into Peter's eyes. Can you imagine that look? Betrayal,

pain, compassion, and love skewered Peter to his soul. He wept bitterly. But as always with Jesus, our darkness is not without hope.

One morning after His resurrection, Jesus found Peter and some of the disciples fishing. Maybe they wanted the comfort of familiar things, but Jesus wasn't willing to leave them in their old life. They didn't recognize Him. "Throw your net to the right side," He said. Perhaps jarred by a memory, John shouted, "It's the Lord." And for the second time in his life, Peter jumped out of a boat to be closer to Jesus.

After breakfast Jesus and Peter walked along the beach, the weight of Peter's conscience slowing his steps. Jesus asked, "Simon son of John, do you truly love Me more than these?" Pain clenched in Peter's chest. "Yes, Lord, You know that I love You." "Feed My lambs," Jesus said. Twice more Jesus asked, "Do you love Me?" Three denials. Three professions of love. Three commands to minister. Peter was restored. (Luke 5:10; 22:54–62; John 13:36–38; 18:15–18, 25–27; 21.)

Do you respond to others with law and rules or love and grace? Only one of these transforms.

Lord Jesus, restorer of my soul, forgiver of my betrayals, You know that I love You. Strengthen my faith so that I can encourage others. Amen.

Know Your Enemy

But I am afraid that just as Eve was deceived by the serpent's cunning, your minds may somehow be led astray from your sincere and pure devotion to Christ.
2 Corinthians 11:3 niv

Pastor A. W. Tozer once told his Chicago congregation, "It is a delightful thing when you know that you are close enough to the adversary that you can hear him roar! Too many Christians never get into 'lion country' at all."* Tozer wasn't encouraging his congregants to go on an African safari. He was talking about spiritual lion country. First Peter 5:8 says, "Be sober, be vigilant; because your adversary the devil, as a roaring lion, walketh about, seeking whom he may devour."

A lion's roar can be heard up to five miles away. If you hear it, keep your wits about you and your eyes open. Satan is stalking you, and the apostle Paul warns us to learn his ways so we don't end up prey. Lions roar to let others know they own this patch of dirt. It terrifies their prey. But they also use it to communicate with others and rally straying lions—a chilling thought that Satan is rallying his forces against us. Satan may be described as a roaring lion in this verse because he's proclaiming his rule over our land. First John 5:19 tells us that our world is under the enemy's control. So wake up, Christian; you live in lion country.

Lions hunt mostly under the cover of night, stalking their prey from dense cover where their sandy coats camouflage three-hundred-pound bodies. Their most successful hunts are of single prey separated from the herd, weak or unaware. But lions are also opportunists with great patience. They will attack in the heat of the day if the chance presents.

Satan also prefers to hunt from cover. He is a devious and cunning murderer masquerading as an angel of light (2 Corinthians 11:14). He lied to Eve in the garden of Eden and has been lying ever since. "He was a murderer from the beginning. . .there is no truth in him. . .for he is a liar, and the father of it" (John 8:44). He hurls accusations against you and attacks your mind (Revelation 12:10). Beware of the voices of shame in your head that would separate you from God and your Christian family.

Study your enemy well so that you can find him crouching in the grass. Know his tactics, and you will be an overcomer!

Lord, give me wisdom and discernment to recognize Satan's attacks so I can resist him. In the powerful name of Jesus, amen.

---

*A. W. Tozer, Tozer Speaks, vol. 1 (Camp Hill, PA: WingSpread, 2010).

Interrupted Life

A man's heart deviseth his way:
but the LORD directeth his steps.
PROVERBS 16:9

They say if you want to hear God laugh, tell Him your plans. He may not laugh, but if our plans sound anything to Him like a five-year-old attempting to launch her paper rocket into space by setting it on fire, maybe He does chuckle. It's wise to hold your plans loosely, because God may be slipping you His to-do list.

C. S. Lewis wrote, "The great thing, if one can, is to stop regarding all the unpleasant things as interruptions of one's own or real life. The truth is of course that what one calls the interruptions are precisely one's real life—the life God is sending one day by day. What one calls one's real life is a phantom of one's own imagination."* Friend, God has a special purpose for each of your days! We like to think we own our time, and if we could just do what we wanted, we would reach our goals. But God says, "There are many devices in a man's heart; nevertheless the counsel of the LORD, that shall stand" (Proverbs 19:21). We make a lot of plans, but God thinks bigger than we do. He wants us to surrender our lives to His will—then we will be living the real life He has for us.

Moses' quiet shepherding life was interrupted when God told him to go and lead Israel out of bondage. Paul's entire life course was reversed when He encountered Jesus. A fervent persecutor of Christians, Paul was on His way to Damascus to arrest more followers of the Way when Jesus turned him from prosecutor to preacher. Jesus was often interrupted by needy people. But it wasn't an inconvenience for Him to do His Father's business. How often do we see the work God has for us as secondary to our own plans, or even an annoyance?

Instead of writing your to-do list as the sun pops over the horizon, try asking God what business He has for you today. Scripture says, "Commit thy works unto the LORD, and thy thoughts shall be established" (Proverbs 16:3). The Hebrew word *commit* here means "to roll; to transfer what is rolled away from oneself to another." Roll the heavy weight of your plans onto God's capable shoulders. Discover the lessons and blessings He sends trimmed in the wrappings of interruptions. Will you allow God's purpose to cut in on your life?

God, what do You want me to do today?
Show me Your plans. Open my spiritual eyes to
see the work of Your hands. I want to help. Amen.

*C. S. Lewis, *The Collected Letters of C. S. Lewis,* vol. 2, ed. Walter Hopper (San Francisco: HarperSanFrancisco, 2005), letter to Arthur Greeves on December 20, 1943.

Blessings

*Oh how great is thy goodness,
which thou hast laid up for them that fear thee.*
PSALM 31:19

A pastor stands at the podium as a giant white projector screen slowly unfurls behind him. A large purple dot sits smack-center on the snowy field. He silently stares out at the crowd. Whispering hums across the sanctuary. Finally, he asks, "What do you see?" A few brave members call out, "A big purple dot!" The pastor dips his head and turns to look at the screen. "And what else?" Silence flows over the audience because the only thing on that screen is a purple circle. Finally someone answers, "A huge white screen?"

"Exactly!" The pastor motions for the next slide and a small key appears at the bottom. It shows that white signifies "God's blessings" and purple signifies "everything else."

We're surrounded by and drowning in God's blessings every day, but we too often choose to focus on the purple dot. Our stress and busyness distract us from the blessings we already have from God. While we are longing for a bigger house, a new car, and a long tropical vacation, we forget to pause and thank God for the roof we live under or the beauty of His creation that sprouts up right outside our door. And whether we're healthy or struggling with disease, we often forget to thank Him for the breath we breathe. That we live is a miracle only He can accomplish.

God isn't minimizing or ignoring our problems, but He

does want us to keep them in the proper perspective. The apostle Paul said to "be careful for nothing; but in every thing by prayer and supplication with thanksgiving let your requests be made known unto God" (Philippians 4:6). The Greek word translated here as "be careful" means "to be anxious about." We're commanded not to be anxious but rather to pray.

In the middle of that verse is a short, easily missed phrase: "with thanksgiving." When you're talking with God about your needs and fears, don't neglect to thank Him for His goodness. If you examine your life and can't see anything that you believe merits blessing status, remember that God gave up His Son for you. An innocent and beloved Son was beaten and crucified to take your place—to restore your relationship with a holy, just, and loving God.

There's also an amazing by-product of this prayer-with-thanksgiving process. God promises that "the peace of God, which passeth all understanding, shall keep your hearts and minds through Christ Jesus" (Philippians 4:7). God's peace will watch and protect your heart as a sentinel guards the castle walls.

God, You've blessed me beyond measure. Even if I had nothing and lived day by day, You died to give me life. You died for me. Thank You. In Jesus' name, amen.

Stripped Bare

*Search me, O God, and know my heart: try me,
and know my thoughts: and see if there be any
wicked way in me, and lead me in the way everlasting.*
PSALM 139:23–24

Old furniture often has awesome potential. Good bones, you might say. It was built with excellent craftsmanship to last. Sometimes haggard pieces that look like they're headed for the burn pile, when refinished, are the most charming. But bringing these lovelies back to life requires more than just a new coat of finish.

Before anything can be done, the peeling layers have to come off. It's incredible that something as abrasive as sandpaper, when scrubbed repeatedly over the surface of the wood, can produce a soft, smooth face. A layer of wood will be lost to get beneath the stain that has soaked into the grain, or just to erase deep scars. And the new finish won't adhere to dry, dead wood. So any gray, exposed areas have to go too, revealing the bright fibers underneath.

Prayer can be a dangerous thing. David's prayer in Psalm 139:23–24 is one to be uttered with care: "Search me, O God, and know my heart: try me, and know my thoughts: And see if there be any wicked way in me." If we invite God to comb the depths of our actions and motives, He will be most discerning. Don't doubt that He will bring up anything in your life that isn't glorifying to Him.

But part of prayer is listening—an all but lost art in today's "me culture." If you talk at God in a constant stream, there's no space in your monologue for His input. So listen well. Open your spiritual ears, and you will hear His voice. Jesus said, "He calleth this own sheep by name, and leadeth them out. . . The sheep follow him: for they know his voice" (John 10:3–4). Sheep spend their lives in the presence of their shepherd; his voice is familiar to them. They trust his gentle cadence and follow his leading. Do you desire to know Jesus' voice? Then be present with Him. Get into your Bible and study His life. Know Him, and you will know His voice.

Petition God to examine your heart, and He will take on the project of refinishing your life. Be prepared to lose a little of your flesh—your pride, selfishness, greed, discontent, unkindness, anything that doesn't originate with the heart of God—when He starts stripping your layers. But rejoice, beloved, in the process. Because with the final stroke of His brush, your life will be remade.

Heavenly Father, search me. Lay bare my motives.
Strip away my sin and teach me to heed Your voice.
In Jesus' precious name, amen.

Less of You

*But they that wait upon the LORD shall renew their strength;
they shall mount up with wings as eagles; they shall run,
and not be weary; and they shall walk, and not faint.*

ISAIAH 40:31

How did you see your life playing out when you were a little girl? Did you dream of a husband and children, a beautiful home where you would nurture and grow your babies? Or did you plan a career—something that filled you to the brim and defined your life? And if it happened to pay well, then success would truly be yours. Everyone has a picture of their ideal future pinned to the halls of their imagination.

But as the years pass, have you grown weary in dream chasing? The luster of raising children can dim a bit after a few years of sleeplessness. Jobs bring stress, and bills pile up. Kids add exhaustion and packed schedules. Sometimes the good things can get covered in the avalanche of obligations and desires. Admit it, striving to make things happen can leave us haggard women with bad attitudes.

In her book *Chasing Slow*, Erin Loechner tells of some advice she received from her surfing instructor after failing to master her board: "Stop relying on your strength. The water is here for you. It's stronger than you are. Let it do the work. Try again this time with less you and more water."*

If you question the direction you're running and struggle after something that's not fulfilling your deep needs, maybe your dreams aren't lining up with the things God has planned

46

for you. Maybe He's trying to get your attention through your discontent and exhaustion. The book of Isaiah says, "They that wait upon the LORD shall renew their strength; they shall mount up with wings as eagles; they shall run, and not be weary; and they shall walk, and not faint" (40:31).

After hearing her teacher's advice, Erin wrote, "I paddle and wait. . . . A wave comes to me, and it carries me, and then I am above it, onto it, on the cusp of something heavy and light and deep and wide, and I am crouching, then standing, then riding to shore."† Maybe you need more God and less you in your dreams. Maybe it's time you stop trying to do life in your own power and wait for God to move and just go with Him. His strength can carry you over struggles and through pain. You will accomplish far more riding His will than you ever could alone.

*God, help me to see Your plan for my life
instead of chasing after selfish desires. Amen.*

*Erin Loechner, *Chasing Slow* (Grand Rapids: Zondervan, 2016), 47.
†Ibid.

Letting Go

Trust in the LORD with all thine heart;
and lean not unto thine own understanding.
PROVERBS 3:5

Jochebed painstakingly wove papaya stems into a basket and carefully tarred it. The life of her child rested on the basket's ability to shelter her son from the water. In a desperate attempt to save his life after Pharaoh's order that all Hebrew baby boys be thrown into the Nile, she cradled her precious three-month-old in the basket, and in a sense obeyed Pharaoh's order when she placed it in the reeds along the Nile. She must have been so scared to trust her precious baby boy to a flimsy reed basket.

The dangers of the Nile River are numerous—sixteen-foot crocodiles, vicious hippos, and at least ten species of venomous snakes inhabit the waters and banks of the Nile. But Jochebed didn't toss her son in a basket and launch it down the moving currents of the Nile. At great danger to herself and family, she had already defied Pharaoh's order and hidden her son for the first three months of his life. But too soon for her mother's heart, hiding was no longer an option. The danger to his survival grew with the strength of his cries.

Probably knowing that Pharaoh's daughter favored this spot on the river, Jochebed set her baby's basket in the reeds close by and likely tasked Miriam to watch over her brother (Exodus 2:4), cautioning her to watch for dangers. It might have even been her plan to retrieve him and try again the next day if the princess didn't come down to the river. But Pharaoh's daughter did come, and she felt compassion for the baby. Miriam seized the opportunity to offer her mother's services as a wet nurse. God protected her son and gifted Jochebed with more time to hold her child—and even payment for her services!

This wasn't the first time God had delivered His people through a vessel coated with tar and pitch. At God's direction, Noah built a watertight ark. Inside these boats was security. And today our security rests in Jesus. Jochebed and Noah trusted God to be their refuge. Do you trust God with the precious things in your life—your kids, job, husband, or dreams—enough to release them to His hands, even in the face of uncertainty? Psalm 62:8 says, "Trust in him at all times; ye people, pour out your heart before him: God is a refuge for us." His plans are beyond the scope of our understanding, but trust in His goodness, friend. Make Him your refuge.

Father God, Jochebed trusted her helpless baby to Your master plan. And You gifted her with more time to mother him and delivered a nation through him. Give me the kind of trust that finds refuge in You alone. Amen.

Looking Back

*But now, after that ye have known God, or rather are known
of God, how turn ye again to the weak and beggarly
elements, whereunto ye desire again to be in bondage?*

Galatians 4:9

The glory days. Reminiscing often leaves us yearning to recapture happy moments gone by. But have you ever revisited something you loved as a kid and been underwhelmed by the experience? Growth and maturity have a way of altering our perspective, but a twinge of nostalgia can at times sour our present experience.

The fertile Nile valley may have been home to the Israelites, but they were enslaved under the oppressive rule of Pharaoh, who worked them mercilessly to weaken them into subservience and murdered their children in the name of population control. Then Moses arrived to shepherd them out of slavery and into a new life of freedom.

God said, "Ye have seen what I did unto the Egyptians, and how I bare you on eagles' wings, and brought you unto myself. Now therefore, if ye will obey my voice indeed, and keep my covenant, then ye shall be a peculiar treasure unto me above all people: for all the earth is mine: and ye shall be unto me a kingdom of priests, and an holy nation" (Exodus 19:4–6).

But in spite of God's proof of His awesome power by sending ten plagues that one by one toppled the Egyptian gods they had worshipped, splitting the Red Sea, and defeating Pharaoh's chariots with the crash of a wave—while Moses was on top of Mount Sinai receiving God's instructions, the

Israelites still looked back to what they'd lost in Egypt instead of ahead to what God promised to make them—His treasure above all people.

God wanted to transform the Israelites into His holy and chosen nation so they could demonstrate His greatness and love to the world, so that "in thee shall all families of the earth be blessed" (Genesis 12:3). He had promised their forefather Abraham that his descendants would become a great nation.

Through Jesus we all have become a part of this family of blessing. We are no longer slaves but daughters with an inheritance (Galatians 4:7–9). The Israelites returned to worshipping their Egyptian idols even after God revealed their idols' worthlessness. What sins or idols from your past do you look back on with longing? Do you truly desire bondage over blessing?

Father, may I never long for the chains of my past. Instead, fill me with a wholehearted desire to obey Your Word and keep Your commands. May I throw off the sins that used to entangle me and never look back. Make me a new person in You—a daughter who pleases You. In Jesus' name, amen.

Work in Progress

For our conversation is in heaven; from whence also we look for the Saviour, the Lord Jesus Christ: who shall change our vile body, that it may be fashioned like unto his glorious body, according to the working whereby he is able even to subdue all things unto himself.

PHILIPPIANS 3:20–21

A sculptor scrutinizes her finished work. Her trained eye snags on small mistakes and a few less-than-graceful lines here and there. Minor things that the casual viewer will overlook. It's the best she can do with this medium, and she's satisfied with her art despite its subtle flaws. She lays aside her tools and steps back to admire the beauty she's created.

God is the potter to our clumsy lump of unformed clay. "O LORD, thou art our father; we are the clay, and thou our potter; and we all are the work of thy hand" (Isaiah 64:8). We are works of art shaped and formed by the hands of a loving Potter with an eye for beauty. His fingers move over us, removing the excess and contouring us into the image of His Son. Soft clay is moldable and yields under His expert touch.

But unlike human artists, He continues to perfect His work. He won't stand aside one day and say, "Well, that's the best that can be done with this one." He is never satisfied with our flaws! Instead, He will continue the good work He started in us, forming us into Christlike beauty, until the day He returns to finish His work: "Being confident of this very thing, that he which hath begun a good work in you will perform it until the day of Jesus Christ" (Philippians 1:6). He won't rest until we are "sincere and without offence. . .being filled with the fruits of righteousness, which are by Jesus Christ, unto the glory and praise of God" (Philippians 1:10–11).

Are you yielded to His touch? Or are you resisting the shape His gentle, transforming hand is moving you toward? If the clay of your heart has become hard, drink deeply of your precious Savior's love until it moisturizes and softens your soul. The Artist who paints stunning sunsets and chiseled majestic mountains is also working to fashion your heart into a thing of beauty.

Thank You, Lord, that You don't leave me where I am. You are constantly moving me toward You and Your truth. Help me to continue to have eyes that see and ears that hear so Your work may be perfected in me daily. Make this the prayer that begins my days. Fix my eyes on You. Let me dwell on everything that is spectacular about You so You may renew my mind and bend my heart toward You and Your love! Amen.

Open the Eyes
of My Heart

That the God of our Lord Jesus Christ, the Father of glory,
may give unto you the spirit of wisdom and revelation in the
knowledge of him: the eyes of your understanding being
enlightened; that ye may know what is the hope of his calling.
EPHESIANS 1:17–18

The danger of reading God's Word is that it can change your perception of reality. And once your spiritual eyes have been opened, there's no going back to a life of ignorant bliss.

In the film *The Matrix* the human race has been captured by machines and their minds enslaved in an artificial reality. A computer hacker named Neo is given a choice by legendary outlaw Morpheus. Take the blue pill and he can go home ignorant of the real world around him. Take the red pill and he will know the truth of his reality. "Let me tell you why you're here," Morpheus says. "You're here because you know something. What you know you can't explain, but you feel it. You've felt it your entire life, that there's something wrong with the world."

When Neo asks Morpheus what truth he's missing, Morpheus says, "That you are a slave, Neo. Like everyone else you were born into bondage. Into a prison that you cannot taste or see or touch. A prison for your mind."* The truth is we, too, are born into slavery. Dead in our sins. And Satan, the great deceiver, doesn't want us to wake up to the reality of our bondage. "It's harmless," he whispers, when in truth it's lethal. "For the wages of sin is death" (Romans 6:23).

Satan imprisons our minds and cloaks his chains of sin in a numbing fog of pleasure and entertainment. He substitutes shallow relationships on social media for real community, vicarious living through video games for the good work of kingdom living, and self-gratification for the joy of our salvation. But we can refuse this pattern and God will renew our minds (Romans 12:2). In His rich mercy, He makes us alive in Christ "even when we were dead in sins" (Ephesians 2:5). We're called to a higher standard of living—holiness. And that requires us to identify and ruthlessly cut sin out of our lives.

Don't settle for deception. May your reality be shaken and the eyes of your heart opened to the danger of sin and the power of God's great love. May your spiritual vision pierce the veil of this temporary existence and the real world of eternity with Jesus snap into focus.

Lord, Satan would imprison me in a pattern of sin and deaden my spiritual eyes to Your truth and life. Give me the spirit of wisdom and revelation and enlighten my spiritual senses so I can truly live. In Jesus' name, amen.

The Matrix, directed by Lana Wachowski and Lilly Wachowski (Warner Bros., 1999), DVD.

Crazy Risk

When thou passest through the waters, I will be with thee;
and through the rivers, they shall not overflow thee.
ISAIAH 43:2

Many rivers have a dam and lock system that allows watercraft to navigate river obstructions like shallow sandbars or rapids. The lock chamber has movable gates at each end. Boats enter one side and the water level is either raised or lowered so the vessels can skirt impassable waters by traveling through the lock.

The surface upstream of the dam's spillway is smooth as polished glass until the water breaks over the dam. Here the force of the current is unmasked. As water slides over the edge, it becomes a churning mass of turbulence that crashes at the base of the dam. The roar of the water and the power of its movement are both awesome and terrible to behold. The thought of being caught in such a flow is terrifying.

But the scene reminds us that many people *are* caught in dangerous waters. Around us exists a writhing mass of humanity, suffering in the midst of pain and hard situations and hopelessness. And the cry of their death throes is deafening. But most of the time, whether it's a recent divorcée or an orphan child, we might say, "Oh, that's sad." We might even thank God that we aren't caught alongside them but not once consider the possibility of sticking even a pinky toe into the raging flood of their pain. We forget that we were spared to rescue others. Instead, we turn aside to the lock, where the waters are gently lowered, and continue on our way, backs to the roiling boil of the river behind us.

And you might be thinking, *But that's crazy! Jumping into someone else's problems and messes and pain is risky.* But what is our faith without risk? Yes, surrendering to God is risky. Radically loving other people is risky.

But God doesn't leave us without promise. Isaiah 43 says, "Fear not: for I have redeemed thee. . . When thou passest through the waters, I will be with thee; and through the rivers, they shall not overflow thee. . . . Thou wast precious in my sight. . .and I have loved thee" (vv. 1–4). Whether you struggle in a current of pain or throw off caution to help another, you are precious to God. He is with you. The rough waters won't swallow you.

God, I thank You for rescuing me. For never leaving me.
For loving me. Lead me into a better life of crazily loving
others. Help me to remember that You are with me,
especially in the hard times. Show me the suffering ones
around me. Soften my heart toward them and fill me
with Your love for them. In Jesus' name, amen.

Powered by the Spirit

Thine, O Lord is the greatness, and the power, and the glory, and the victory, and the majesty: for all that is in the heaven and in the earth is thine; thine is the kingdom, O Lord, and thou art exalted as head above all.

1 Chronicles 29:11

"I could never do that," you say. I could never be that missionary, that youth leader, that mom of a special-needs child—those are sacrificial jobs that leave you wondering at the source of their strength and the depth of their love.

But the truth is you *can* do it too. Anyone can. "How?" you ask. The Holy Spirit wants to invade your life. He wants to occupy your body and use it for kingdom gains. You can do hard things joyfully because *you* don't have to! The awesome truth of walking in the Spirit's power is that *He* does the heavy lifting through you. Your inner self might be cranky, tired, and weak, but the Holy Spirit is joyful, energetic, and strong! And He imbues you with all of His power.

Change your outlook by adopting Paul's prayer for the Ephesian believers. Make it your daily request:

For this cause I bow my knees unto the Father of our Lord Jesus Christ, of whom the whole family in heaven and earth is named, that he would grant you, according to the riches of his glory, to be strengthened with might by his Spirit in the inner man; that Christ may dwell in your hearts by faith; that ye, being rooted and grounded in love, may be able to comprehend with all saints what is the breadth, and length, and depth, and height; and to know the love of Christ, which passeth knowledge, that ye might be filled with all the fulness of God. Now unto him that is able to do exceeding abundantly above all that we ask or think, according to the power that worketh in us, unto him be glory in the church by Christ Jesus throughout all ages, world without end. Amen. (Ephesians 3:14–21)

You can do life "strengthened with might by his Spirit," "rooted and grounded in love," and "filled with all the fullness of God"! Sister in Jesus, the next time you are down, worn out, and feeling unappreciated or overwhelmed, stop and pray. Activate the Spirit's power that will strengthen you and make you an overcomer. "But ye shall receive power, after that the Holy Ghost is come upon you: and ye shall be witnesses unto me" (Acts 1:8).

Holy Spirit, overwhelm me with Your power. Fill me with the fullness of God's limitless love and strength until they spill out of me onto every person I encounter. You, God, can do greater things than I could ever imagine! In Jesus' powerful name, amen.

Do the Small Stuff

*He that is faithful in that which is least is faithful also in much:
and he that is unjust in the least is unjust also in much.*
LUKE 16:10

"Do I have to play this scale again?" Somehow the fantasy idea of pounding out a piano masterpiece never includes the mundane practice of finger-stepping up and down the keyboard over and over. . .and did I say *again*? The glory of being a concert pianist appeals to many, but few are willing to put in the thousands of playing hours required for mastery. And there's no shortcut to training your fingers to dance across the keys.

Learning to follow Jesus doesn't have a shortcut either. Want the abundant life God promises? Do the small stuff—every day. Start by craving the pure spiritual milk of God's Word so you can mature in your faith. And once you have tasted God's goodness, like a hungry child you will squall for more (1 Peter 2:2–3). But babies aren't satisfied with milk forever. As your spiritual maturity increases, you will be ready to digest the "strong meat" of scripture (Hebrews 5:12).

Pray continually about everything (1 Thessalonians 5:17). God wants you to talk to Him. And He has stuff to say to you. Prayer positions you to recognize your need for God's provision—not just materially but spiritually. We need His grace and strength each day. Do you recognize God's voice when He speaks to you? It takes practice to discern His voice from your own and the enemy's. Look for God's characteristics in what you hear. His voice is never harsh or criticizing or mean. He speaks with kindness and gentleness and love.

We have a choice. The prophet Jeremiah said to stand at the crossroads and ask for the good way, then walk down that road toward rest for your soul (6:16). So how do we determine which is the good way? Micah 6:8 says, "He hath shewed thee, O man, what is good; and what doth the LORD require of thee, but to do justly, and to love mercy, and to walk humbly with thy God?" That is no small feat. But it comes down to a choice—your choice. Will you obey?

Jesus said, "He that is faithful in that which is least is faithful also in much: and he that is unjust in the least is unjust also in much" (Luke 16:10). What little things have you been neglecting? Daily prayer? Reading the Word? Tithing?

God, forgive me for ignoring the daily habits of faith
that sometimes feel repetitive and unimportant.
Bless me with a greater desire to be obedient in
every way, no matter how small. Amen.

In the Company of Silence

Give ear, O my people, to my law:
incline your ears to the words of my mouth.
PSALM 78:1

Introverts have a fond relationship with silence. Some people need entertainment and stimulation and activity, but while the introspective do enjoy good conversation, their idea of a relaxing day is more in line with sitting on the front porch, coffee in hand, with hours of solitude—to think.

Mark 1:35 says: "And in the morning, rising up a great while before day, he went out, and departed into a solitary place, and there prayed." This verse is often used as an encouragement for early morning quiet times, which many of us do prefer—often because that is the only time we can put the "quiet" in our time with God. But we can glean more than a wake-up call from this verse. Arguably more important than the time of day was the location: a solitary place. He sought out the silence so He could listen to God.

Mother Teresa said, "I always begin my prayer in silence, for it is in the silence of the heart that God speaks, so we need to listen. For, it is not what we say, but what God says to us and through us that matters. Prayer feeds the soul—as blood is to the body, prayer is to the soul, and it brings us closer to God."* The discipline of listening seems old-fashioned today. We want sound bites of information, and our interactions have become the "Look at me!" of social media instead of "How are you?" Impatience and self-absorption have hijacked our prayer lives as well.

Evading external noise isn't too difficult, but sometimes quieting the voice of self within is the more gargantuan task. That inner voice starts chattering and bounces from our to-do list to our grocery list in seconds flat. But with practice and focus we can muzzle our inner magpie.

Jesus' prayer life models a pattern of entering silence to converse with God and then responding to His voice. In his book *The Spirituality of Listening*, Keith R. Anderson calls this listening "*with* another person in relationship and curiosity. It is a listening that can wait for the presence of another to emerge. Some call it meditative or contemplative listening, others name it holy listening or even prayer; it is a way of life in which we actively listen for what God might reveal."[†] Without listening there is no conversation.

Heavenly Father, speak to me. I'm listening for Your voice;
my ears are inclined to Your words. Amen.

---

*Mother Teresa, *A Simple Path* (New York: Random House, 1995), 7.
†Keith R. Anderson, *The Spirituality of Listening: Living What We Hear* (Downers Grove, IL: InterVarsity, 2016), 173.

Into the Desert

*Ye shall know that I am the L ORD your God, which bringeth
you out from under the burdens of the Egyptians.*
EXODUS 6:7

Before delivering the Israelites from slavery and the bustle and
wealth of Egypt, God promised them this:

> *I am the L ORD, and I will bring you out from
> under the burdens of the Egyptians, and I
> will rid you out of their bondage, and I will
> redeem you with a stretched out arm, and
> with great judgments: and I will take you to
> me for a people, and I will be to you a God:
> and ye shall know that I am the L ORD your
> God, which bringeth you out from under the
> burdens of the Egyptians. And I will bring
> you in unto the land, concerning the which
> I did swear to give it to Abraham, to Isaac,
> and to Jacob; and I will give it you for an
> heritage: I am the L ORD. (Exodus 6:6–8)*

God had pledged Canaan to the Israelites. So why did He
lead them to the desert instead of the promised land? In the
scripture, a verse rests between their delivery from slavery and
their inheritance of Canaan—in it He promises to make them
His own and be their God: "Ye shall know that I am the L ORD
your God." He led them into the bleak emptiness and stark

solitude of the desert because He wanted them to encounter Him. The desert experience reflects the poverty of spirit we all must enter into before we can see God (Matthew 5:3).

But they were looking back into Egypt instead of ahead to where they were going—to His plan. God took them into the desert to strip them of the distractions and false security of their former life and rebuild them into a nation who would serve Him—to teach them to rely on Him alone.

In his book *The Way of the Heart*, Henri Nouwen describes the desert's school: "Solitude is the furnace of transformation. Without solitude we remain victims of our society and continue to be entangled in the illusions of the false self. . . . Solitude is the place of the great struggle and the great encounter—the struggle against the compulsions of the false self, and the encounter with the loving God who offers himself as the substance of the new self."* God took Israel into the desert to change the way His people thought and restore them to Himself.

What deserts have you passed through? Did you complain about your circumstances, or did you encounter God there?

Lord, keep me from complaining in the wilderness of hardship. Instead, help me to find You there. Amen.

---

*Henri Nouwen, *The Way of the Heart: Desert Spirituality and Contemporary Ministry* (New York: Ballantine, 1991), 15–16.

Dust

He knoweth our frame;
he remembereth that we are dust.
Psalm 103:14

We come from humble beginnings. After God had spoken the world and its creatures into existence, He planted a garden for His final and most special workmanship. "Then the Lord God formed a man from the dust of the ground and breathed into his nostrils the breath of life, and the man became a living being" (Genesis 2:7 NIV). Minus God's breath, we are nothing but dead and lifeless dirt.

We often take great pride in our genealogies, bragging about important relatives and the pivotal events our forebears may have participated in. As if their achievements might somehow improve our own. But God remembers our ultimate source: just dust.

Flawed as we are, we often struggle in habitual sin and missed goals. Over and over we fall short of the mark. And you might wonder how God can continue to put up with our unkept promises and faltering faith through the generations.

The prophet Hosea lived in the final days of Israel's northern kingdom before the Assyrians conquered Israel's land. The Israelites were once again worshipping Canaanite deities, and Hosea was called by God to live in painful symbolism. The Lord told Hosea to take an adulterous wife and have children of unfaithfulness with her, because Israel had committed adultery by being unfaithful to the Lord. Ouch! But God had plans to show Himself faithful.

Hosea had three children with his wife, Gomer, who chased after other lovers and returned to Hosea unsatisfied. Then the Lord told Hosea, "Go yet, love a woman. . .yet an adulteress, according to the love of the LORD toward the children of Israel, who look to other gods, and love flagons of wine" (Hosea 3:1). By this point, Gomer's lifestyle had apparently led to slavery, because Hosea bought her back for fifteen pieces of silver and some barley (Hosea 3:2). Even in the face of her flagrant rejection of his love, Hosea remained faithful.

Despite our determination to turn from Him, God's great compassion is stirred toward us (Hosea 11:7–8) because "he knoweth our frame; he remembereth that we are dust" (Psalm 103:14). Just as Hosea paid the slave price for his wife, Jesus is the One "who forgiveth all thine iniquities. . .who redeemeth thy life from destruction; who crowneth thee with lovingkindness and tender mercies" (Psalm 103:3–4).

God doesn't treat us as we deserve. Even after we've cheated on Him with worldly pleasure, His love for us remains steadfast.

Lord, forgive my unfaithful ways when I put my own comfort, schedule, or desires first. Redeem me from the destruction I often bring upon myself. Crown me with Your mercy. Your compassion and kindness and love overwhelm me. In Jesus' name, amen.

Heart of Forgiveness

Love your enemies.
MATTHEW 5:44

Nelson Mandela was imprisoned twenty-seven years for resisting South Africa's racist apartheid system. Upon his release from prison, he said, "As I walked out the door toward the gate that would lead to my freedom, I knew if I didn't leave my bitterness and hatred behind, I'd still be in prison."* Mandela led the way for reconciliation after apartheid; he even invited one of his former prison guards to dinner and said it "reinforced my belief in the essential humanity of even those who had kept me behind bars."†

In Rwanda nearly a million people were murdered during the 1994 genocide—when the Hutus began slaughtering the Tutsis. As part of a national effort toward reconciliation, the nonprofit Association Modeste et Innocent promotes reconciliation between genocide perpetrators and survivors, where after months of counseling the perpetrators formally request forgiveness. In a powerful *New York Times* photo-essay, some of these survivors were photographed in almost unimaginable poses. One woman's hand rests on the shoulder of the man who killed her father and brothers. Another woman said this of the man who killed her child: "He came to ask me pardon. I immediately granted it to him because he did not do it by himself—he was haunted by the devil. . . . Now, I would rather treat him like my own child."‡

These modern-day tales of incredible forgiveness seem to echo God's mission for the prophet Jonah. Nineveh was the capital city of the Assyrian Empire—a feared enemy of Israel who had committed heartless cruelty. And God commissioned Jonah to take to them His message of reconciliation. But Jonah resisted. And we look into his heart and see ourselves—afraid, selfish, spiteful, and proud. The mercy shown by those Rwandan survivors stands in stark contrast to Jonah's unforgiveness.

But God's call to Jonah—and to apartheid victims and genocide survivors—is no different from His call to us. From the cross, Jesus cried, "Father, forgive them; for they know not what they do." To you He says, "*That person who wronged you? Forgive them. That person who hates you? Love them.*" In Jonah we see our own internal resistance to hard-to-love people. It requires true humility to recognize that our sins balance theirs on the scales of God's justice.

Can you forgive like that?

Lord, it's hard to grasp Your brand of mercy. Help me see the depth of my own failings and the greatness of Your grace, so I can also forgive. Amen.

*Trudy Bourgeois, "The Greatest Gift—To: You and I, From: Nelson Mandela," *Huffington Post Blog*, December 19, 2013, updated February 18, 2014, http://www.huffingtonpost.com/trudy-bourgeois/the-greatest-gift_b_4469297.html.
†Dominic Gover, "Nelson Mandela: Four Acts of Forgiveness That Showed South Africa Path Away from Apartheid," *International Business Times*, December 6, 2013, updated July 1, 2014, http://www.ibtimes.co.uk/nelson-mandela-forgiveness-south-africa-apartheid-528153.
‡Susan Dominus, "Portraits of Reconciliation," *New York Times Magazine*, April 6, 2014, https://www.nytimes.com/interactive/2014/04/06/magazine/06-pieter-hugo-rwanda-portraits.html.

Abide

Whoever claims to live in him must live as Jesus did.
1 John 2:6 niv

Have you ever experienced the joy of meeting someone who seemed to completely understand you? You think, *I like her. She gets me!* Over the years, your conversations seem to exist outside of time and your shared lives compound until she understands every crevice of your soul, and you hers. But what if you had never gone out of your way to know her? Instead of a soul sister, she would be a mere acquaintance you exchange smiles with in the grocery aisle.

When Jesus calls us to come to Him, He means for us to stay. Jesus said, "I am the vine, ye are the branches: He that abideth in me, and I in him, the same bringeth forth much fruit: for without me ye can do nothing" (John 15:5). The word *abide* means "to stay (in a given place, state, relation, or expectancy), to continue, to dwell, to endure, to be present, to remain, to tarry." Are you present with Jesus? How often are we not present even with one another? Oh, we're in the same room, but our focus is elsewhere.

Andrew Murray wrote, "You have wondered what the reason could be, that with such a Saviour, so mighty and so loving, your experience of salvation should not have been a fuller one. The answer is very simple. You wandered from Him. The blessings He bestows are all connected with His 'Come to me,' and are only to be enjoyed in close fellowship with Himself."* Jesus didn't mean for us to come to Him for one brief moment—to receive salvation, experience His awesome grace and power, and then go on about our lives, nodding to Him on Sunday.

Instead, Jesus is saying that every minute from now on, in the work you do, in your rest, in your fun, in your joy and pain, be present with Him. Tarry in friendship with the Lord and your joy will be complete.

What does this friendship look like in practice? The apostle John wrote that if we say we are abiding in Christ, that we should be walking as Jesus walked—in love. Unless we remain with Jesus, our lives will not bear the Spirit's fruit of love, joy, peace, patience, gentleness, goodness, kindness, faithfulness, and self-control (Galatians 5:22–23, 25). Is Jesus the husband of your soul, or a mere acquaintance?

Jesus, fill me with desire to seek Your presence. I want to be present with You—always. My good Friend, strengthen me to walk in the most excellent way of love. Nourish my soul through abiding in Your vine. Amen.

---

*Andrew Murray, *Abide in Christ* (Apollo, PA: Ichthus Publications, 2014), 11.

Eyes Forward

Remember ye not the former things, neither consider the things of old. Behold, I will do a new thing; now it shall spring forth; shall ye not know it? I will even make a way in the wilderness, and rivers in the desert.
Isaiah 43:18–19

Moving forward is like crossing monkey bars. You have to let go with one hand at some point to move forward. Paul says much the same thing in Philippians 3:13–14: "Brethren, I count not myself to have apprehended: but this one thing I do, forgetting those things which are behind, and reaching forth unto those things which are before, I press toward the mark for the prize of the high calling of God in Christ Jesus."

Satan will try to remind you of all the mistakes that litter your past as you reach out for the future God has for you. "You blew it," he'll whisper. "You've missed the boat of God's will for you. There's no catching it now." But remember, Satan is a liar. Forget what is behind you. Paul says to throw off the sin that entangles. We're no longer slaves to it. And God doesn't hold our pasts against us. His grace covers all.

Don't buy the lie that one wrong choice will ruin God's plan for your entire life. Give God some credit for creativity in working His plan! God can still redeem our bad choices and work His will despite our mistakes along the way. After all, if He used only perfect people, not much would get done. And we aren't mere cogs in the gears of His plan. God loves each one of us individually. But His plan *is* bigger than just you. You would have to be self-absorbed to think otherwise. His ultimate goal is saving the world by the blood of His Son, new life, and a new way of living for everyone.

But if you refuse to take part and don't fulfill His individually crafted purpose—the reason God placed you here—it could cause pain and loss both in your life and in the lives of those you were meant to help. Christ has spared us and showed us what real love is by His own example so we can love others. There could be an injustice you were uniquely positioned to right or a wound your specific brand of compassion could soothe. All that would be lost without your yes. Will you forget what is behind and tell Him yes when He asks for your help?

God, keep my focus on You. May my love for You be shown by my obedience. Don't let my past or the world's promises of comfort and prosperity discourage me from saying yes to anything You ask of me. Amen.

A Good God

This then is the message which we have
heard of him, and declare unto you, that
God is light, and in him is no darkness at all.
1 JOHN 1:5

"Congratulations! You've won an all-expense-paid vacation to Hawaii!" the overeager voice bubbles out of your phone. Naturally your skepticism is piqued. "What's the catch?" you ask. Because things that are too good to be true usually are, right?

Within every believer lives a split personality of good and evil—the influences of the Holy Spirit and our flesh are at war within us: "For the flesh lusteth against the Spirit, and the Spirit against the flesh: and these are contrary the one to the other: so that ye cannot do the things that ye would" (Galatians 5:17). We want to please God but have trouble denying the self-focused desires of our hearts. The apostle Paul wrote, "For I know that in me (that is, in my flesh,) dwelleth no good thing: for to will is present with me; but how to perform that which is good I find not. For the good that I would I do not: but the evil which I would not, that I do" (Romans 7:18–19).

Because of this internal battle, our motives aren't always pure. We can do things that look good on the outside but for all the wrong reasons. Some side benefit to us is fueling our actions, whether it is pride, personal gain, or power. We can't be fully trusted. And too often we project our limitations onto God. Our world, tainted with sin, has taught us that nothing is as good as it sounds, so maybe God isn't either.

But 1 John 1:5 says that "God is light, and in him is no darkness at all." So we're not dealing with a shifty God—His character has no taint of impurity. Instead, "we're dealing with Light. He's revealed Himself. Laid Himself bare in the open and in a light so clean and bright only His holiness could withstand it. And He's not just in the light, He is the light."* And that means God is good, wholly good, nothing but good. We can trust Him because He isn't trying to hide His agenda from us. "God doesn't have any dark folds in His cloak."†

"Oh how great is thy goodness, which thou hast laid up for them that fear thee; which thou hast wrought for them that trust in thee before the sons of men!" (Psalm 31:19).

God, it's easy to think of Your goodness in human terms. But You are good all the way through. There's no rotten core to taint Your motives. Thank You for Your absolute goodness. In the name of Jesus, amen.

---

*Kelly Minter, *What Love Is* (Nashville: LifeWay, 2014), 27.
†Ibid.

It's War

For though we walk in the flesh, we do not war after the flesh: (For the weapons of our warfare are not carnal, but mighty through God to the pulling down of strong holds).
2 CORINTHIANS 10:3–4

Our enemy prefers either to blind us to all spiritual conflict or recruit us to his side. In the classic *Screwtape Letters*, C. S. Lewis wrote, "There are two equal and opposite errors into which our race can fall about the devils. One is to disbelieve their existence. The other is to believe and feel an unhealthy interest in them. They themselves are equally pleased by both errors and hail a materialist or a magician with the same delight."* How much easier to cut down clueless civilians wandering onto a battlefield when they're not even aware there's a war. Or better yet to deceive them into fighting for the enemy.

The apostle Paul gave his own war rally when he described our spiritual harassers: "For we wrestle not against flesh and blood, but against principalities, against powers, against the rulers of the darkness of this world, against spiritual wickedness in high places" (Ephesians 6:12). We are involved in a struggle that is not of this world, and we can't use human resources to win.

But God has designed effective weapons and given us His battle plan through scripture. But if we leave active duty for a comfortable civilian life, we're defenseless and likely to become casualties. Jessie Penn-Lewis wrote in her book *War on the Saints*, "The chief condition for the working of evil spirits in a human being, apart from sin, is passivity, in exact opposition to the condition which God requires from His children for His working in them."[†] Don't be lulled into thinking you have no need for armor. God calls us to take an active part in the spiritual defenses He has provided: "Finally, my brethren, *be strong in the Lord, and in the power of his might. Put on* the whole armour of God, that ye may *be able to stand against* the wiles of the devil" (Ephesians 6:10–11, emphasis added).

Satan may run this planet, but he isn't our ruler. When we received Christ, God "delivered us from the power of darkness, and hath translated us into the kingdom of his dear Son" (Colossians 1:13). But as long as we are on earth, we're in Satan's territory. As foreigners in a hostile nation, we need protection from the enemy's deception. Armor up, soldier!

God, thank You for pulling me from the enemy's camp.
Give me battle savvy to daily step into my armor
and stand firm against Satan. Amen.

---

*C. S. Lewis, *The Complete C. S. Lewis Signature Classics* (New York: Harper-Collins), 183.
†Jessie Penn-Lewis, *War on the Saints,* 9th ed. (New York: Thomas E. Lowe, 1973).

Buckle Up

Lead me in thy truth, and teach me: for thou art the God of my salvation; on thee do I wait all the day.
PSALM 25:5

The *Merriam-Webster Collegiate Dictionary* defines truth as "sincerity in action, character, and utterance." And Jesus said, "I am the way, the truth, and the life" (John 14:6). So Jesus embodied the truth about God in His actions, character, and words. The Bible says He *is* the Word (John 1:1, 14), God's mouthpiece to proclaim the truth about Himself to us. Apart from God's choice to tell us about Himself, we lowly humans have no way of knowing our living God.

Today's philosophy says to define your own truth. Whatever works for you must be your truth. But we already know the person of truth, and it's not us! Francis Schaeffer said, "Today not only in philosophy but in politics, government, and individual morality, our generation sees solutions in terms of synthesis and not absolutes. When this happens, truth, as people have always thought of truth, has died."* As Christians we must protect ourselves with God's truth. Ephesians says to buckle the belt of truth firmly around our waists (6:14). It is vital to our defense because the belt holds the other pieces of body armor in place.

If we know the truth about who God is and who we are in Him, we aren't without defense when Satan tries to sell us a pack of lies. "The devil. . .abode not in the truth, because there is no truth in him. When he speaketh a lie, he speaketh of his own: for he is a liar, and the father of it" (John 8:44). Because his primary weapon is to lie, our belt of truth is under a constant barrage of attack. But we can stand firm against him by holding every thought, every action, every compulsion up to the measuring stick of God's character. Ask yourself, Is this something God would say or do? Because if Satan can convince us there's truth in his lies, then he also controls our actions in that area. Because action follows thought.

Jesus prayed for His followers on the night before His crucifixion: "I pray not that thou shouldest take them out of the world, but that thou shouldest keep them from the evil" (John 17:15). And what was Jesus' plan for our defense against evil? "Sanctify them through thy truth: thy word is truth" (v. 17). Study His Word. Know the truth. Defend yourself.

God, I buckle Your truth firmly around me.
Reveal the enemy's sneak attacks and bring the words
of Your truth to mind when I need them. Amen.

---

*Francis Schaeffer, *Christian Quotes*, http://christianquotes.org/author /quotes/176.

Armor Plated

The night is far spent, the day is at hand: let us therefore cast off the works of darkness, and let us put on the armour of light. Let us walk honestly, as in the day; not in rioting and drunkenness, not in chambering and wantonness, not in strife and envying. But put ye on the Lord Jesus Christ, and make not provision for the flesh, to fulfil the lusts thereof.

ROMANS 13:12–14

The apostle Paul says that we must "stand therefore. . .having on the breastplate of righteousness" (Ephesians 6:14). We're given Christ's righteousness when we accept God's grace and repent of our sins at salvation. At this point, God no longer sees our filthy rags of sin when He looks at us; instead, we are justified through the blood of Christ. The breastplate we heft is Christ's righteousness, not ours. "And be found in him, not having mine own righteousness, which is of the law, but that which is through the faith of Christ, the righteousness which is of God by faith" (Philippians 3:9).

We all sin. Even as a follower of Jesus, you will not be perfect. But when Satan aims his accusations against you and claims you aren't good enough to be a Christian, remember that you are now dressed in the white robe of Jesus' righteousness. And God's response to Satan's charges against us? "Who shall lay any thing to the charge of God's elect? It is God that justifieth" (Romans 8:33).

Our command as believers is also to imitate Jesus—to love others unselfishly and follow scripture's commands to walk by the Spirit and not gratify the desires of our flesh (Galatians 5:16). The apostle Paul says in Ephesians to "walk as children of light: (for the fruit of the Spirit is in all goodness and righteousness and truth). . . . Walk circumspectly, not as fools, but as wise, redeeming the time, because the days are evil" (5:8–9, 15–16).

Sin in your life is like a Trojan horse for Satan. If we live right, we don't give Satan a foothold in our lives. But when we engage in sinful behavior, we hand him an opportunity to attack from inside our defenses. First Thessalonians 5:8 says, "Let us, who are of the day, be sober, putting on the breastplate of faith and love." Exercise self-control and point to your new white dress when Satan tries to discourage and depress you by stealing your joy and hope. If you have sinned, throw it off and walk in obedience.

Lord, guard my actions so that the enemy has no grip on my life. Reveal my hidden sins so that I can repent. I will not be ashamed anymore because I am garbed in Your righteousness. Amen.

New Shoes

Great peace have they which love thy law:
and nothing shall offend them.
PSALM 119:165

Roman soldiers transformed their sandals into military footwear with shoe tacks. Their hobnailed shoes provided protection and superior grip for marching and combat. Roman soldiers also encased their legs in brass greaves, or shin armor, to protect them from the enemy's galltraps, sharp sticks, or other obstructions meant to injure their feet and legs and render them ineffective in battle.

Ephesians says that our feet should be "shod with the preparation of the gospel of peace" (6:15). In his commentary on Ephesians, Matthew Henry quotes Dr. Daniel Whitby: "That you may be ready for the combat, be shod with the gospel of peace, endeavor after that peaceable and quiet mind which the gospel calls for. Be not easily provoked, nor prone to quarrel: but show all gentleness and all long-suffering to all men, and this will certainly preserve you from many great temptations and persecutions, as did those shoes of brass the soldiers from those galltraps."

The gospel brings peace in many forms—with God, with ourselves, and with others. Paul says that the feet of those who share the gospel message are beautiful because they bring good news (Romans 10:15).

Part of that good news is that through Jesus we now have peace with God. Without Him we were enemies of God

(Romans 5:10), but now "being justified by faith, we have peace with God through our Lord Jesus Christ" (Romans 5:1). The peace of God also rules in your heart and gives you an attitude of serenity even in the midst of your battles. God loves us and asks that we trust Him with our anxiety and promises that His peace will guard our hearts and minds (Philippians 4:6–7).

Christians are all members of one body, the church (Colossians 3:15–16). But Satan applies the divide-and-conquer strategy—backbiting, gossip, pride. He likes nothing better than to split up the family of God through unforgiveness. If you want to frustrate his efforts, become a peacemaker who sows fellowship and reconciliation (Romans 14:19).

When a brother or sister in Christ offends you, recognize that your battle is not with them; it's with the enemy who delights in shattering your relationships. Experience victory by subscribing to Proverbs 19:11: "It is his glory to pass over a transgression." Too often we revel in our offenses. As God's children, we share unity in the Spirit even if we don't always have a meeting of the minds. And we have the promise that "the God of peace shall bruise Satan under your feet shortly" (Romans 16:20).

God, I have the peace of knowing that I am reconciled to You. Keep my heart humble and my forgiveness ready. Sharpen my peacemaker skills. Amen.

Accessorize with Faith

Through faith we understand that the worlds were framed by the word of God, so that things which are seen were not made of things which do appear.
HEBREWS 11:3

What would Captain America be without his nigh-impenetrable Vibranium shield to protect him from his enemies' weapons? Fictitious Vibranium is the rarest metal on earth. Stronger than steel and a third of its weight, it is completely vibration absorbent. And God has also given us a game-changing weapon of defense—our faith.

Hebrews 11:1 says faith is "the substance of things hoped for, the evidence of things not seen." It is our confidence in God's promises to us. Our faith grows with our knowledge of God. And our knowledge of God comes through His Word. "Faith cometh by hearing, and hearing by the word of God" (Romans 10:17). As we daily walk with God and learn more about His ways, our trust in His promises will grow, as will the protective power of our shield.

Roman legionaries carried large, curved rectangular shields called scutum, which they raised in testudo—the tortoise formation. The soldiers formed a shell by overlapping their shields above and in front to protect them from arrows. Scripture says that our shield of faith has the power to quench the enemy's fiery darts as well (Ephesians 6:16). Satan launches vicious emotional attacks as flaming darts of temptation, anxiety, and hardship that could ignite and fill us with fear. In his book *Making Spiritual Progress*, Allen Ratta writes, "If you have lived very long you know all about fiery darts. They are like cruise missiles that wind their way through our defenses. They hit with a bang and start a fire. We can feed the fire into an inferno by nursing and rehearsing the unkind words that were spoken. We can let ourselves be blackened with bitterness. I like Paul's approach: pick up the shield of Faith. It is no wonder that he emphasizes 'above all'—pick up that shield!"*

Faith doesn't mean that we irrationally ignore reality; it just means that our eyes have been opened to our eternal reality as opposed to being blinded by our immediate circumstances. Fear is the opposite of faith, and our faith in God wipes out anxiety's power over us. Jesus promised, "My peace I give unto you: not as the world giveth, give I unto you. Let not your heart be troubled, neither let it be afraid" (John 14:27). Our belief in God's ultimate control and submission to His will allows us to exhibit the traits of faith—peace, confidence, courage, and trust.

God, increase my faith and trust in You in the face of problems that might otherwise leave me cowering in a corner. Amen.

---

*Allen Ratta, *Making Spiritual Progress* (Downers Grove, IL: InterVarsity, 2014), 124.

Fierce Hat

*That through death he might destroy him that had the power
of death, that is, the devil; and deliver them who through
fear of death were all their lifetime subject to bondage.*
HEBREWS 2:14–15

The fear of being controlled by outside forces has at times led humanity into ridiculous practices—including strapping on aluminum foil hats. The earliest recorded use in fiction of an anti-mind-control foil deflector beanie is Julian Huxley's *The Tissue-Culture King*, written in 1926. Others through the years have picked up this interesting habit, believing that their foil headgear would shield their brains from extraterrestrial interference, mind control, and mind reading.

While alien mind control isn't something to fret about, we do have an enemy who seeks to influence our thoughts. Satan has mastered the art of psychological warfare because spiritual battles are won or lost on the battlefield of your mind. If Satan can pilfer your hope, he can convince you that victory is impossible. Devoid of hope, soldiers no longer press forward in confidence but scatter in a retreat of fear.

Soldiers' helmets protect a vital part of their anatomy—their heads. In Paul's illustration, the helmet of salvation protects your mind from spiritual attack. Your salvation in Christ ensures your eternal victory over Satan. Regardless of whether you suffer losses on the battlefield from time to time, Satan cannot remove you from the hand of God: "And I give unto them eternal life; and they shall never perish, neither shall any man pluck them out of my hand" (John 10:28).

God has crushed Satan's rule of fear by taking away the power of death and giving us eternal life with Him through the crucifixion and resurrection of Jesus. "God is my salvation; I will trust, and not be afraid. . . . Fear not: for I have redeemed thee, I have called thee by thy name; thou art mine" (Isaiah 12:2; 43:1).

Beware of the doubting voice that questions the reality of your salvation in Jesus or your position as God's child, especially if you have given in to temptation, fear, or anxiety. Take heart, you are a daughter of the King of kings, and nothing can separate you from His love, including demons and spiritual powers (Romans 8:35–39). Satan knows he's the big loser in this war, but if he can put the kibosh on your immediate victory in today's battle over sin, then maybe you'll despair and doubt God's power and ability to save you eternally. Never surrender your hope. Forget the foil hat; your position in Christ secures your ultimate win over Satan.

God, protect my mind from the enemy's deception.
He wants me to doubt You and everything You have
said. Keep my spiritual vision sharply focused on
Your power, authority, and protection. Amen.

Wield Your Sword

It is written, Man shall not live by bread alone, but by every word that proceedeth out of the mouth of God.
MATTHEW 4:4

No soldier with an inkling of self-preservation walks onto a field of conflict without his weapon. But it seems that many believers are doing just that. We fall to temptation because we either won't admit we're at war with spiritual forces or we just don't bother to pick up our sword. We meet his attack empty-handed and end up on our backsides in the dirt.

Our only offensive weapon listed in God's armor is the spoken Word of God (Ephesians 6:17). Paul calls it the sword of the Spirit to remind us that this battle is spiritual and can't be fought in our own strength. The sword originates with the Spirit, and we need the Holy Spirit's power and the truth of God's Word to stand firm.

We have a lot of rationalizations for why we don't read and memorize the Bible: "It's too hard." "I'm too busy." "I can search it on my Bible app; why do I need to know it?" And the enemy is more than pleased to strip you of your weapon by convincing you that it's not worth your time, too difficult, and old-fashioned. But memorized scripture will return when you need it—when the devil tries to pass off one of his lies as truth.

When Satan tempted Jesus in the desert, He combated the enemy's falsehoods with three words: "It is written." The blazing truth of God's Word sends Satan running back into the darkness. The relationship between memorizing scripture and our ability to resist temptation is well founded. Not only was it the tactic Jesus threw at Satan, but Psalm 119:11 says, "Thy word have I hid in mine heart, that I might not sin against thee."

Satan is a wily foe with millennia of human observation behind him, but don't credit him with divine attributes. Satan cannot read your mind or see the future. His knowledge of God's plans is limited to what God has said. The Bible gives examples of God knowing a person's thoughts and Jesus knowing others' thoughts, but never of Satan doing the same (Psalm 139:4; Mark 2:6–8). In fact, in the book of Job, Satan's comments about Job were limited to outward observations of his behavior (Job 1:9–11; 2:4–5). So he can't eavesdrop on your internal thoughts. But that is not to say that he can't guess at your motivation through observing your actions. That's why it's important to resist Satan outwardly through spoken words of scripture and put him on the run.

Lord, hone the edge of my weapon through scripture memorization. Your Word is powerful and sharper than a two-edged sword. Amen.

Pray Always

Men ought always to pray, and not to faint.
Luke 18:1

While the sword of the Spirit is the only offensive weapon listed as armor, prayer is arguably our most effective defense against the enemy. Before going to the cross Jesus prayed in anguish, His sweat, like drops of blood, fell to the ground (Luke 22:44). That same night He warned Peter about his upcoming trials: "Pray so that you will not fall into temptation" (v. 46 NIV). Too often we see prayer as an emergency blanket instead of as our first line of defense. Jesus came back from His prayers in the garden of Gethsemane and found Peter and the other disciples sleeping. "Peter, are you sleeping? Couldn't you keep watch for one hour?" What is your prayer life like? Can you keep watch for even an hour?

After instructing us in gearing up for combat, Paul wrote, "Praying always with all prayer and supplication in the Spirit, and watching thereunto with all perseverance and supplication for all saints" (Ephesians 6:18). It echoes Jesus' "Get up and pray, Peter." Pray in the Spirit. All the time. Both Jesus and Paul warn us to be alert in prayer.

In his book *The Bondage Breaker*, Neil Anderson writes:

One of the most dramatic deliverances I have observed happened in a man who was a high priest in the upper echelons of Satanism. Six months after he was set free he gave his testimony in our church. At the close of his testimony I asked him, "Based on your experience on 'the other side,' what is the Christian's first line of defense against demonic influence?"

"Prayer," he answered forcefully. "And when you pray, mean it. Fervent prayer thwarts Satan's activity like nothing else."*

God is willing to move on our behalf, but like the disciples, too often we abandon our watch. James wrote, "Yet ye have not, because ye ask not" (James 4:2). And because we are not God, we don't always know what to say. But we have reinforcements: "The Spirit helps us in our weakness. We do not know what we ought to pray for, but the Spirit himself intercedes for us through wordless groans" (Romans 8:26 NIV). The word *help* in this verse is used in the sense of "to help in obtaining; to take hold with another (who is laboring)."†

Do you have an hour a day for conversation with God? Diligently pray. The Spirit will labor with you, and God will show up in mighty ways!

◦◦◦

Lord, change me into a woman of prayer. Open my spiritual eyes so I can see where my prayers are needed. Give me strength to maintain the watch. Amen.

*Neil T. Anderson, *The Bondage Breaker* (Eugene, OR: Harvest House, 1993), 86.
†*Thayer's Greek Lexicon, Blue Letter Bible,* s.v. "synantilambanomai," https://www.blueletterbible.org/lang/lexicon/lexicon.cfm?Strongs=G4878&t=KJV.

Tempted

There hath no temptation taken you but such as is common to man: but God is faithful, who will not suffer you to be tempted above that ye are able; but will with the temptation also make a way to escape, that ye may be able to bear it.

1 CORINTHIANS 10:13

Temptation has been around since the garden of Eden—it happens when we're attracted to something outside of God's bounds. Eve saw the fruit, and it looked delicious and pretty, and Satan told her it would also enhance her understanding. Sounds good, right? Except God had already hammered in His NO TRESPASSING sign. But Eve chose her own desires over God's will and committed the first sin. Temptation itself is not the sin—it's the action of giving in that follows.

When they were confronted by God about their disobedience, Adam and Eve trotted out the classic finger-pointing excuses that we still employ. "Totally not my fault, dude." But if it weren't for our own internal desires, temptations would no longer be—well, tempting. So the ultimate blame rests solely on our shoulders. "Every man is tempted, when he is drawn away of his own lust, and enticed" (James 1:14).

So don't throw the blame around. We make our own choices. And don't accuse God either; that's not His style (James 1:13). Temptations are a tool of the enemy to misdirect your worship. Satan doesn't really care if you worship him; he just doesn't want you to worship God. And he'll bait his trap with anything you find attractive.

Jesus was also tempted, but He kicked sin in the teeth (Hebrews 4:15). He is called the second Adam because He resisted temptation. He toppled Satan's enticements with the Word of God. His arguments began with "It is written." Knowing scripture saves us from being blinded by our desires and Satan's lies like Eve was. So what do we do when confronted by temptation? Run (2 Timothy 2:22; 1 Corinthians 6:18). And remember that our failures don't change God's love and mercy toward us (1 John 1:9; Proverbs 28:13).

Have you ever taken the bait that all good things are sin? But good doesn't equal sin. Satan would have us swallow the same lie Eve did—that God was keeping something good from her. But James says not to be fooled: "Every good gift and every perfect gift is from above, and cometh down from the Father of lights, with whom is no variableness, neither shadow of turning. Of his own will begat he us with the word of truth, that we should be a kind of firstfruits" (James 1:17–18). God's pleasure is that you become the cream of His crop!

Lord, when temptations look desirable, remind me that sin brings death, but Your ways bring life. Amen.

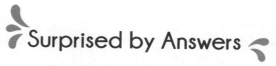

Surprised by Answers

*The effectual fervent prayer of
a righteous man availeth much.*

JAMES 5:16

Peter was awakened by a sharp pain in his side. King Herod had arrested him during Passover, and tomorrow he would stand for public trial. A light in his prison cell blinded his sleep-heavy eyes, and he pressed his hand to his sore ribs, surprised by the freedom of his arms. Was it morning already? He had hoped for a little more time before his trial. Peter rubbed his eyes and looked around. His chains curled along the floor like dead serpents, shackles open. Confused, he decided his earlier thoughts of liberation must be giving him strange dreams.

"Quick, get up!" The sharp command rang with authority. The angel standing in his cell seemed real enough. *Imminent death provokes the most vivid dreams*, Peter thought.

"Put on your clothes and sandals," the angel said. Peter glanced at the two guards he'd been chained to, one on either side. They appeared oblivious to his wild dreams, so Peter obeyed. "Wrap your cloak around you and follow me." Peter trailed the angel past the two sentries guarding the entrance. The iron gate leading to the city swung open on silent hinges as if propelled by an invisible hand, and they strolled out of prison and onto the streets of Jerusalem. Peter turned to the angel. He was gone!

Peter cut a glance to the left and right. The quiet city night was real. God had rescued him from execution! Sandals slapping softly on the street, Peter hurried to the home of John Mark's mother, Mary.

He knocked on the outer gate. "It's me, Peter! Let me in!" Peter kept knocking, and after some time a group of believers opened the gate. "Rhoda told us you were here, Peter, but we didn't believe her!"

On the night before His crucifixion, Jesus had told Peter to pray, and it seems that the first-century believers had heeded His warning—unlike Peter in the garden of Gethsemane, they weren't asleep on their watch. Instead, a large group of them were holding a night prayer vigil. But surprised by their answered prayer, they told Rhoda she was out of her mind.

Sometimes we ask God for things, not really expecting Him to move. But "this is the confidence that we have in him, that, if we ask any thing according to his will, he heareth us: and if we know that he hear us, whatsoever we ask, we know that we have the petitions that we desired of him" (1 John 5:14–15). Prayer works. Pray boldly and believe. Your answer may already be knocking.

God, sometimes I underestimate Your awesome power. Give me faith that when I pray according to Your will, You will answer. Amen.

One Thing

Be sober, be vigilant; because your adversary the devil, as a roaring lion, walketh about, seeking whom he may devour.
1 PETER 5:8

"It's okay if you don't have time to read your Bible. Having young kids is intense. Jesus understands you're tired and busy." You may have heard similar advice. And if you don't have children, just fill in the blank with whatever overwhelms your life. It sounds reasonable on the surface. After all, caring for others is a noble and righteous cause. But heed this advice at your own risk. When you're exhausted and run ragged, that is exactly the time when you need to hear God's encouraging voice speaking words of life into your chaos.

Friends, we have an enemy among us. He prowls the grass like a lion, looking to cull the weakest from the herd. Beware when your intimacy with God wanes because you've neglected the relationship. If you wander from the safety of the Shepherd's reach, you're an easy target. Weak and alone, there's no doubt you'll be devoured.

It's so very easy to mix up our priorities. When compared to the demands from husbands and jobs, children and family, a little quiet breathing room with God can start looking like a luxury instead of a necessity. But consider: If you're not drawing from the deep well of God's strength, what is fueling you? The shallow pool of your own sufficiency will not last.

Martha chose busyness over relationship when Jesus came to visit. She rushed around her kitchen, seeing to every detail and probably sweating through her clothes. Her irritation spiked when she saw her sister, Mary, sitting at Jesus' feet, learning with the men. Martha thought Mary was shirking her duty and pointed this out to Jesus. But she didn't get the response she was looking for. "Martha, Martha, thou art careful and troubled about many things: but *one thing* is needful: and Mary hath chosen that good part, which shall not be taken away from her" (Luke 10:41–42, emphasis added).

Mary chose the one thing that mattered, while Martha was busy losing her cool over many inconsequential things. Sitting at the feet of Jesus is not a luxury; it's a must-have. That's not to say that you should lock yourself in a room with your Bible and ignore responsibility. But it might mean that you need to weigh on an eternal scale the things that occupy your time. Do you lose yourself in television, social media, or Pinterest? Are you overcommitted to extracurricular activities or work? Anything. *Anything* can become a stumbling block to your relationship with Jesus. All you have to do is put it before Him.

Jesus, kindle an unquenchable desire within me to be with You. Expose to me the enemy's distractions. Amen.

The Pursuit of Contentment

But godliness with contentment is great gain.
For we brought nothing into this world,
and it is certain we can carry nothing out.
1 TIMOTHY 6:6–7

Does your stress arise from a contentment problem? We often battle between what we have and what we think we need—or what our televisions or friends inform us we must have. The rampant consumerism surrounding us often ends in an unquenchable desire for more.

The tiny-house movement is oddly fascinating. It's no longer comprised only of hippie vagabonds but a growing number of people who seek simplicity and freedom by living in four hundred square feet or less. The apostle Paul said that he had discovered the secret of contentment, whether he was hungry or fed, living in plenty or imprisoned in rags, and said, "I can do all things through Christ which strengtheneth me" (Philippians 4:13).

Contentment doesn't usually jump to mind when we read this verse. Out of context, it prompts images of power and success. But Paul isn't saying that we will always "win" in the world's eyes. Rather, he has discovered something better—that no matter whether we're suffering or living at the top of our game, we can bear up under all circumstances, good or bad, because the almighty God of the universe will lend us His strength. We can be satisfied right where we are because God will carry us through.

Jesus told His disciples in Matthew not even to worry about food. He said to let the pagans run after those things, but that their heavenly Father already knows all their needs. "But seek ye first the kingdom of God, and his righteousness," He said, "and all these things shall be added unto you" (Matthew 6:33).

God desires that we pursue His kingdom with at least the same zeal that we shop the aisles of our favorite outlet store. That we expand His kingdom with the same focus we use to fill our homes with beautiful things. He wants us to throw off sin and worldly pursuits to follow Him, to love one another as we love Him.

Neither the pursuit of minimalism nor consumerism will satisfy apart from God. John Stott wrote, "Life on earth is a brief pilgrimage between two moments of nakedness. So we would be wise to travel light. We shall take nothing with us."* The true key to freedom is to ask, *Whose empire am I building? Have I gained any heavenly treasures? Or is everything I value found here on earth?*

Heavenly Father, thank You for generously providing for my needs. You strengthen me in every circumstance. I don't want the passion for stuff to drive me. Plant in me the longing to seek Your kingdom first, before my self-focused desires. Amen.

---

*John Stott, *The Radical Disciple* (Downers Grove, IL: InterVarsity, 2010), 21.

God's Bigness

*Lift up your eyes on high, and behold who hath created
these things, that bringeth out their host by number.*
Isaiah 40:26

Ninety-three billion light-years across—scientists say that's the size of our *observable* universe. At six trillion miles per light-year, that math is mind-boggling, and that's just the part we can see. Scientists don't know how big the universe is; it could be infinite—and it's expanding. An article in *Wired* magazine says that to imagine the size of the universe, "place a penny down in front of you. If our sun were the size of that penny, the nearest star, Alpha Centauri, would be 350 miles away. Depending on where you live, that's very likely in the next state (or possibly country) over. . . . At this scale, the Milky Way galaxy would be 7.5 million miles across."* It's too hard to bend our mind around that many zeroes.

But God is there, containing and surrounding it all. Psalm 139 says, "If I take the wings of the morning, and dwell in the uttermost parts of the sea; even there shall thy hand lead me, and thy right hand shall hold me." And "if I ascend up into heaven, thou art there: if I make my bed in hell, behold, thou art there" (vv. 9–10, 8).

God holds all that massive space we can't begin to comprehend in the palm of His hand: "My right hand hath spanned the heavens" (Isaiah 48:13). Isaiah 40 says, "Who hath measured the waters in the hollow of his hand, and meted out heaven with the span, and comprehended the dust of the earth in a measure, and weighed the mountains in scales, and the hills in a balance? . . . The nations. . .are counted as the small dust of the balance: behold, he taketh up the isles as a very little thing" (vv. 12, 15). Our world is dust on His scale, not weighty enough to tip its balance.

And the immensity of God is that He made it all, and He holds our universe together: (Psalm 8:3; Colossians 1:17). Isaiah 40 says, "It is he that sitteth upon the circle of the earth, and the inhabitants thereof are as grasshoppers; that stretcheth out the heavens as a curtain, and spreadeth them out as a tent to dwell in. . . . To whom then will ye liken me, or shall I be equal? saith the Holy One" (vv. 22, 25).

Lord, why do I bother with fear when You are bigger than the vastness of our universe? God, You are very great! Amen.

---

*Adam Mann, "How to Picture the Size of the Universe," Wired, December 6, 2011, https://www.wired.com/2011/12/universe-size/.

Your Choice

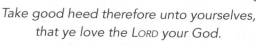

Take good heed therefore unto yourselves,
that ye love the LORD your God.
JOSHUA 23:11

Life is a journey marked with crossroads. Yes, your choice to follow Jesus is like choosing to go east or west on your trip, but all the small choices after that are like determining which roads you will take—paved highways or scenic backcountry byways. Maybe you'll end up at a dead end, a wrong turn, or in some potholes. So evaluate your potential paths wisely.

The question, "Will you obey God or go your own way?" isn't asked of you only a single time, but every day, and usually multiple times every day. How you react when someone offends you is your choice. Will you kill them with kindness or glare daggers? Don't be a passenger. You can take charge of your emotions and choose self-control over out of control.

Gary Chapman's *The Five Love Languages* tells how we all interpret love differently. Some see love in acts of service, and others find it through affirming words or something else. If you really want to express your love, you need to study others and learn their love language. If your husband interprets love in the language of quality time and you give him gifts, he's not going to be feeling very loved because you're not speaking his language.

Fortunately, we don't have to guess what God's love language is because He told us in His Word. Jesus said, "If a man love me, he will keep my words: and my Father will love him, and we will come unto him, and make our abode with him" (John 14:23). God's love language is obedience.

Joshua was pretty white in the beard by the time the Israelites had conquered most of the promised land. Before he died, he gathered the leaders together for one final encouragement:

> *Be ye therefore very courageous to keep and to do*
> *all that is written in the book of the law of Moses,*
> *that ye turn not aside therefrom to the right hand or*
> *to the left; that ye come not among these nations,*
> *these that remain among you; neither make mention*
> *of the name of their gods, nor cause to swear by*
> *them, neither serve them, nor bow yourselves unto*
> *them: but cleave unto the LORD your God, as ye have*
> *done unto this day. . . . Choose you this day whom ye*
> *will serve.* (Joshua 23:6–8; 24:15)

He advised them to avoid false gods and yield their hearts to the Lord (Joshua 24:23).

Each word and action is a choice. Do yours speak God's love language of obedience? Who will you choose to serve today?

God, show me the idols in my life that rob me of
obedience to You. Give me spiritual wisdom to
choose You with every decision. Amen.

No Substitutes

I am the LORD; and there is none else. I have not spoken in secret, in a dark place of the earth: I said not unto the seed of Jacob, Seek ye me in vain. . . They have no knowledge that set up the wood of their graven image, and pray unto a god that cannot save. . . . Look unto me, and be ye saved.
ISAIAH 45:18–20, 22

A substitute is a thing that takes the place of something else. Buttercream frosting is the best. Its smooth and fluffy texture is a baker's dream for crafting gorgeous desserts, and its sweet, creamy yumminess melts in your mouth, coating your taste buds in heavenly delight. But whipping up the perfect frosting requires the best ingredients. The texture and taste will be ruined if you substitute beet sugar for cane sugar and pull out the margarine instead of real butter. Sure, you end up with frosting, but the quality will suffer.

Our God is the real McCoy. No alternates welcome. Have you ever considered the horror and devastation the Egyptians experienced during the ten plagues? Their land was wrecked, their animals and crops destroyed, their oldest sons dead. But they weren't merely economically ruined; they were spiritually decimated as well. With each new plague, God proved to the Egyptians that their idols were powerless, nothing but weak substitutes, and that He alone is the I AM (Exodus 3:14). His purpose in the plagues was that "the Egyptians shall know that I am the LORD, when I stretch forth mine hand upon Egypt, and bring out the children of Israel from among them" (Exodus 7:5).

The plagues also proved his authenticity to the Israelites before He freed them from slavery—that He is the all-powerful God over any Egyptian idols they may have adopted during their captivity. God displayed His power so that they would know Him, and some of the Egyptians believed and possibly even left with the Israelites during the Exodus (see Exodus 9:20; 12:38).

What substitutes have you put in God's place? Ask Him to show you anything that you've replaced Him with. If you don't think you have time to read His Word, ask Him to reveal what you're substituting there. If your prayer life is nonexistent, what distracts you from conversation with Him?

God, show me any weak substitutes I've replaced You with. Reveal to me the things that I use for comfort and security instead of seeking You. Show me what distracts me from listening to Your voice. I want more of You, God. You are the I Am. There is no other. Amen.

Kinsman-Redeemer

*Arise for our help, and redeem
us for thy mercies' sake.*
PSALM 44:26

Ruth was a kind and virtuous woman, and a Moabite. She didn't have to return to Bethlehem with her Jewish mother-in-law, but she chose Naomi's people and her God as her own. And she was blessed. In Bethlehem, Ruth and Naomi lived in poverty without husbands. So Ruth gleaned in the fields during the barley harvest—widows and the destitute were permitted this to survive.

It just so happened—or God saw to it; don't you love how God leaves it to us to see His work where we will?—that Boaz owned the field Ruth gleaned in and was a close relative of Naomi. He noticed Ruth's loving care for her and said, "A full reward be given thee of the LORD God of Israel, under whose wings thou art come to trust" (Ruth 2:12).

Boaz means "In him is strength." And as a vulnerable widow, Ruth certainly found strength in his care and protection. Boaz was a man of wealth and standing in Israel, and he was also known for his kindness—maybe a result of his mother's influence. Boaz was the son of Rahab, the prostitute who smuggled Hebrew spies out of Jericho and, like Ruth, chose to join them. Boaz told Ruth to stay in his fields where she would be safe and instructed his workers to drop extra grain for her.

One night Naomi sent Ruth to the threshing floor, where

Boaz would be sleeping to protect his harvest, to invoke her right to a kinsman-redeemer—a relative who would buy back sold or lost land, marry the widow, and provide an heir for the dead man. Boaz didn't have to redeem Ruth, but he was qualified by blood and had the means and willingness to do so.

That night Ruth pleaded her case before Boaz: "Spread therefore thy skirt over thine handmaid; for thou art a near kinsman" (Ruth 3:9). The hem was the emblem of rank in Israel, and just as she'd sheltered under the wings of God, Ruth asks Boaz to spread the wings of his garment, representing his protection in marriage, over her. Boaz married Ruth and produced a royal line—their great-grandson was King David, a forebear of Christ.

God has also chosen the poor of this world—the poor in spirit, the oppressed, and the vulnerable. Boaz foreshadows another kindhearted kinsman-redeemer—Jesus! Through His act of redemption, Jesus takes His bride, the church. He was born in human form to share in our weakness and bloodline, and through His perfect obedience to the law, Jesus was able to redeem us, and He willingly laid down His life on the cross.

Jesus, thank You for Your willingness to redeem.
Thank You for Your love and abundant kindness. Amen.

Bondage Breaker

*Stand fast therefore in the liberty wherewith
Christ hath made us free, and be not entangled
again with the yoke of bondage.*

GALATIANS 5:1

Losing sovereignty over your mental state must surely be utter torment. Mary Magdalene understood this helplessness and agony well, and she was totally devoted to her Deliverer.

Mary had once been mastered by something else—something dark. Seven demons resided in her. We don't know how long they tormented her or how it affected her, but seven is a number signifying completion. So it is likely that they fully dominated her mind. When she met Jesus, He drove the demons from her. Her sanity was restored! She was free! Mind clear for the first time in a while, Mary had no doubt of Jesus' authority as the Son of God and her new Master. From then on she devoted her entire existence to Jesus. Mary must have been either of a wealthy family or a wealthy widow, because she followed Jesus and cared for His needs and financially supported His ministry (Mark 15:40; Luke 8:2–3).

When most of His disciples fled, Mary watched Jesus' crucifixion. Her agony must have been acute as she likely heard the hammer's ring against the nails. She watched her gentle and kind Master—yet also the Lord she knew commanded legions of angels and held the power over death and life—willingly submit His life. She stayed by His side until the stone was rolled across the entrance to His tomb.

After the Sabbath, Mary wept in grief outside Jesus' tomb. His body was gone, and she didn't know where. The gardener asked her why she was crying, but she knew only that her Lord was gone.

"Mary." She knew that voice. She knew His tone and inflection infused with compassionate kindness. "Rabboni!" Not a gardener—her Jesus was alive!

It's easy to understand Mary's adoration and total devotion to Jesus. She was truly delivered. Her mind and body were restored to peace after her nightmarish encounter with the enemy.

Jesus said, "If ye continue in my word, then are ye my disciples indeed; and ye shall know the truth, and the truth shall make you free. . . . Whosoever committeth sin is the servant of sin. And the servant abideth not in the house for ever: but the Son abideth ever. If the Son therefore shall make you free, ye shall be free indeed" (John 8:31–32, 34–36). What masters you, my friend? Has the enemy tried to enslave you? Pick up your sword; continue in His Word, and you will know freedom.

Jesus, You delivered Mary and You can deliver me.
Give me strength to continue in Your Word. Amen.

Pray

*The end of all things is at hand: be ye
therefore sober, and watch unto prayer.*
1 PETER 4:7

Your situation is beyond your control. Hopelessness creeps over your soul. No solution presents itself. No help seems imminent. In defeat you say, "I guess there's nothing left to do but pray."

Pray.

Hope stirs in your heart. *Why did I wait so long?*

For a moment you felt alone. While staring an unfixable problem in the face, you blinked, and outward circumstances robbed your inner peace. Satan may come to steal and kill and destroy, but God is never blindsided by unforeseen events. He never wrings His hands thinking, *Oh my, I didn't see that coming!* As we learn to trust God's goodness and believe that He can make a way—just as He split the waters of the Red Sea and cleared a highway to freedom for the Israelites where there was no passage—we can begin to act with maturity of faith instead of reacting with fear and hopelessness.

The apostle Paul wrote that believers should "pray without ceasing" (1 Thessalonians 5:17). We too often pray as a last resort instead of a first line of defense. Instead of slowing to yield to the movement of God, we panic and rush to action, compelled to do something. In our pride and impatience, we seem to have trouble viewing prayer as an active solution instead of a desperate Hail Mary pass as time expires. It's difficult to admit our own inadequacy and ineffectiveness. And the act of prayer requires both humility and surrender.

Jesus told His disciples about a widow who went to an unjust judge asking for justice, and the judge ignored her plea. But she kept going back and asking over and over. Finally, the judge relented just to get rid of her. "Shall not God avenge his own elect," Jesus said, "which cry day and night unto him, though he bear long with them? I tell you that he will avenge them speedily" (Luke 18:7–8). Imagine the mountains a loving God would level if we could be so persistent in merely asking.

At the end of His call for prayer, Jesus asked a question that resonates today: "When the Son of man cometh, shall he find faith on the earth?" (Luke 18:8). Scripture says that at the end of the ages "because iniquity shall abound, the love of many shall wax cold. But he that shall endure unto the end, the same shall be saved" (Matthew 24:12–13). The end of the ages draws ever nearer, friend. If Jesus returned today, would He find you faithful in prayer and loyalty, or has your love grown cold?

Lord Jesus, I want to stand steadfast in prayer. Show me the power of being a prayer warrior in Your kingdom. Amen.

Fellowship of Suffering

*The sufferings of this present time are not worthy to be
compared with the glory which shall be revealed in us.*
ROMANS 8:18

Struggling is important for any growth experience. A story is
told about a boy's pet caterpillar. When the caterpillar formed
a chrysalis, he watched it each day, excited for the butterfly to
emerge. Finally, a small hole appeared. But soon the butterfly
started to struggle. Worried, the boy clipped a bigger hole for
the butterfly to come out quickly. It emerged with a swollen body
and small shriveled wings. He learned later that the butterfly
was supposed to struggle—that as it squeezed through the
tiny opening, it pushed the fluid out of its body and into its
wings. Without the struggle, the butterfly never flew.

Don't buy Satan's lie that if you follow Jesus, He will take
away all your pain and suffering and give you an easy life of
comfort. Jesus loves you too much, friend, to rob you of the
ultimate benefit of your earthly struggle. But Satan would love
to steal your joy and kill your hope and destroy your relationship with God and with other Christians if you let him lie to you
unchecked (John 10:10). Always hold what you hear against the
truth of scripture, which says that Christians must strap on our
armor and prepare for battle. Who needs armor for a life of ease?

Jesus warned His disciples that they would not find accep-
tance from the world: "If the world hate you, ye know that it

hated me before it hated you. If ye were of the world, the world would love his own: but because ye are not of the world, but I have chosen you out of the world, therefore the world hateth you. . . . The servant is not greater than his lord. If they have persecuted me, they will also persecute you. . . . The time cometh, that whosoever killeth you will think that he doeth God service" (John 15:18–20; 16:2). Paul called this sharing the "fellowship of his sufferings" (Philippians 3:10).

Paul wrote that "our light affliction, which is but for a moment, worketh for us a far more exceeding and eternal weight of glory; while we look not at the things which are seen, but at the things which are not seen: for the things which are seen are temporal; but the things which are not seen are eternal" (2 Corinthians 4:17–18). Like the butterfly with its momentary struggle, we suffer temporary trials here for eternal kingdom gains—the reward of a mature faith and everlasting life with Jesus.

Jesus, You suffered for me, and I should not expect an easier road. Show me the spiritual benefits of the hard things You work for my good so I can rejoice in my trials. Amen.

Broken Vessel

God hath chosen the weak things of the world
to confound the things which are mighty. . .
that no flesh should glory in his presence.
1 Corinthians 1:27, 29

A crayon-crazy three-year-old girl begs for more paper, pretty please. Her mom hands her a sheet, but the girl throws it away, crying. Her mom retrieves the paper and finds a tiny word from her forgotten grocery list scrawled in the corner. In her daughter's mind, one small imperfection rendered all that blank potential unusable.

I'm so glad God isn't that picky about His utensils! It's a relief to know that even if we mess up sometimes, we're not tossed away—that God is still willing to push His pen across our tainted life. The apostle Paul was used greatly by God. Yet he called himself chief among sinners (1 Timothy 1:15). Mother Teresa shared Paul's humble self-analysis: "I'm just a little pencil in His hand. Tomorrow, if He finds somebody more helpless, more stupid, more hopeless, I think He will do still greater things with her and through her."* The less we become, the more completely His strength is manifested in our lives (2 Corinthians 12:9–10). Imagine if the pencil fought back. The writer's penmanship would surely suffer. Surrender to His mighty hand, and He will pen His masterpiece.

Friend, have you been tainted? Have you made poor choices, said hurtful words, been in wrong places, and suffered the consequences of a shattered heart, failed relationships—a broken life? Have you felt hopelessness? Despair? Jesus met such a woman by a well. She'd messed up and been outcast, but He restored her through forgiveness, hope, and life—He gave her His living water. And then He wrote His purpose into her life: "And many of the Samaritans of that city believed on him for the saying of the woman" (John 4:39). You don't have to stay where you are, beloved. Jesus still wants you for Himself.

Paul wrote, "In a great house there are not only vessels of gold and of silver, but also of wood and of earth; and some to honour, and some to dishonour. If a man therefore purge himself from these, he shall be a vessel unto honour, sanctified, and meet for the master's use, and prepared unto every good work" (2 Timothy 2:20–21). We've all dishonored God with our actions. But we can become vessels of honor prepared for the good works God has planned for us. What does your life of pain and dishonor gain you? That life isn't worthy of you. Purge yourself of those old acts of sin and become a sanctified vessel in your Father's great house.

Sanctify me, Jesus, so I am ready
for Your good work. Amen.

*Mother Teresa, *Where There Is Love, There Is God*, ed. Brian Kolodiejchuk (New York: Doubleday Religion, 2010), 334.

The House
He's Building

Ye also, as lively stones,
are built up a spiritual house.
1 PETER 2:5

Change can be so constant. You don't even feel a
difference until there is one. It can be so slow that
you don't even know your life is better or worse until
it is. Or it can just blow you away in an instant and
make you something different.*

Life as a House is a film about a broken man and all the broken, hurting people around him. George Monroe spent his life being overcome by an abusive childhood—his drunk father killed his mother in a car accident. The woman driving the other car also died, and her daughter in the backseat was injured. His life is colored by pain—until he finds out he has four months to live and gets fired from his job. The film is filled with disturbing immorality and poor choices made in an attempt to soothe deep pain, but the reality of this very state in the world around us is undeniable.

In a desperate attempt to start anew, George decides to tear down his father's house, a shack sitting on beautiful oceanfront real estate. And then he tells his ex-wife that their drug-addicted teenage son can live with him for the summer. George and his son, Sam, who only helps at first because he desperately needs drug money, begin to build together. And through the building of this house, they begin to love each other. And love changes everything. Not just for them, but for every life connected to theirs as well.

When we come to Jesus with our pain and find life in Him, He wants to tear down the crumbling shack of our old lives and build a spiritual house out of us. Altogether, the Church is like a large spiritual building made out of people who offer spiritual sacrifices by loving God and each other. One stone does not make a building. We need one another—a place to belong and be loved. We need community. God is calling us out of the darkness of our self-absorbed worlds into His marvelous light. He wants to change us into something that we weren't before: "Which in time past were not a people, but are now the people of God: which had not obtained mercy, but now have obtained mercy" (1 Peter 2:4–10).

In the end, George dies and leaves the house to his son. In the last scene, Sam and his mother sit outside a rundown trailer park with a wheelchair-bound woman. "My father built you a house," Sam says. Love someone today. It changes everything.

Heavenly Father, You have built me a house. I've been damaged by this world, but You can make me something different than what I was before. Amen.

Life as a House, directed by Irwin Winkler (New Line Cinema, 2001), DVD.

Into Lion Country

The god of this world hath blinded the minds of them which believe not, lest the light of the glorious gospel of Christ, who is the image of God, should shine unto them.

2 CORINTHIANS 4:4

Days before the Dunkirk evacuation, Winston Churchill faced the possible annihilation of the British Expeditionary Forces. The Allies were quickly being surrounded at Dunkirk, the last port where British forces could be evacuated from Europe. On May 19, 1940, in his first radio broadcast as prime minister, Churchill called the men to valor: "Centuries ago words were written to be a call and a spur to the faithful servants of Truth and Justice: 'Arm yourselves, and be ye men of valour, and be in readiness for the conflict; for it is better for us to perish in battle than to look upon the outrage of our nation and our altar. As the will of God is in Heaven, even so let it be.'"

Churchill gave a sober yet rousing entreaty as the German army was poised to take Dunkirk, and Jesus likewise attempted to bolster Peter's defenses on the eve of great spiritual attack from Satan. Seated around a table, the disciples ate their last Passover meal with Jesus, who knew how their faith was about to be tested. But Peter didn't grasp his precarious position. Jesus tried to shake his spiritual senses awake to the crouching enemy: "Simon, Simon, behold, Satan hath desired to have you, that he may sift you as wheat" (Luke 22:31). Peter was being stalked.

Later on the Mount of Olives, Jesus again warned him: "Pray that ye enter not into temptation" (Luke 22:40). Can you hear

Jesus' intensity? It's as if He's saying, *"Pray, Peter, pray like never before! The enemy prowls like a lion seeking to devour you!"* But heedless, Peter falls asleep. And the predator approaches.

That night Peter is shaken—abandoned prayers lead to the hasty violence of slicing off Malchus's ear and Peter's denial of Christ, not once but three times. The enemy's razor claws leave Peter's heart and confidence in bloody ribbons. Prayer is a vital action. Without it we ignore God's plan and race into the battle fray ignorant of the general's strategy. And the outcome is defeat—our own personal denial of Jesus as we stumble into sin.

But we can learn to stand as Peter did. Lions rarely alter their path of attack: Satan's predictability gives us an edge, and "we are not ignorant of his devices" (2 Corinthians 2:11). In Acts 4, Peter and John were imprisoned, but they refused to stop talking about Jesus, and the religious leaders were astonished at their courage.

If Peter stood firm, so can you.

Lord, show me what You want me to do. Help me to seek You. Protect me from Satan's attacks. Amen.

Now Walk in His Ways

But now being made free from sin, and become servants to God, ye have your fruit unto holiness, and the end everlasting life.
ROMANS 6:22

Our victory over Satan is already on the books. His defeat is final. But true to form as the liar he is, he would convince us that we're still chained in slavery to our sins, that every bad choice and faithless action defines us. First he convinces us that one little lie or one tiny, self-centered decision can't possibly be deadly. "Look around. It's the norm," he says. "You deserve this one small thing for yourself." No sooner do we give in than his tone morphs. "Oh, you've done it now. God can't use you looking like that. Run away while you can, sinner. Selfish. Mean. Dishonest. Jealous. That's you. Don't forget to duck the divine lightning on your way out!"

But the prophet Zechariah had a vision of God throwing Satan's arguments out of court. And Jesus defends us continually against Satan's accusations. His blood on the cross has redeemed us. We've been pulled from the fire; our future is secure (Zechariah 3:1–6). But our rags-to-riches story doesn't end here.

Now God asks that we live out our faith in response to the grace He has showered us with. He asks for our obedience: "If thou wilt walk in my ways, and if thou wilt keep my charge, then thou shalt also judge my house, and shalt also keep my courts, and I will give thee places to walk among these that stand by" (Zechariah 3:7). In calling us to walk in His ways and keep His charge, God is talking about our daily victory over sin. "How shall we, that are dead to sin, live any longer therein? . . . We are buried with him by baptism into death: that like as Christ was raised up from the dead by the glory of the Father, even so we also should walk in newness of life. . . . Let not sin therefore reign in your mortal body, that ye should obey it in the lusts thereof" (Romans 6:2, 4, 12).

Sometimes dying to self is a moment-by-moment decision. At the crossroad of My Way and God's Way, will you declare, "Sin, you don't own me anymore! I've traded up for a new mind that captures every thought and wrangles it into obedience to Christ"? Put sin to death, and like Jesus you will be resurrected to a new life! (Romans 6:4–5).

God, You have clothed me in righteousness and transformed me by renewing my mind. Through the power of Your Holy Spirit, help me to walk in Your ways. Amen.

Beatitudes

Lay not up for yourselves treasures upon earth,
where moth and rust doth corrupt, and where thieves
break through and steal: but lay up for yourselves treasures
in heaven, where neither moth nor rust doth corrupt,
and where thieves do not break through nor steal:
for where your treasure is, there will your heart be also.
MATTHEW 6:19–21

Early in His ministry, the news about Jesus' healings and teaching was spreading. Huge crowds followed Him. So Jesus strolled up a hill and sat down. There He gave His famous Sermon on the Mount, His inaugural address calling all who would be His followers to a new standard of living. The message He shouted was, "Become a new creature. Get a new heart! And the blessing of eternity will be yours!"

He began with a series of eight blessings known as the Beatitudes, which paint a vivid portrait of the Christian counterculture for His hearers. They include, among others, "Blessed are the merciful, for they will be shown mercy. Blessed are the pure in heart, for they will see God. Blessed are the peacemakers, for they will be called children of God" (Matthew 5:7–9 NIV). Jesus is proclaiming that becoming part of His kingdom will radically transform your life. And we can't belong to His kingdom and the world's at the same time.

If we have been transformed by God's grace, we will be merciful. If we have submitted to the Spirit's heart cleansing, we will see God in heaven. If we have accepted the peace God made with us through Jesus, we will share the peacemaking character of our Father in heaven. Because when we truly recognize the poverty of our spirit and mourn our sins and accept God's grace, we will hunger for His righteousness. And our lives will be changed.

Jesus isn't giving us optional characteristics—to be either merciful or meek—instead, He's giving us the ancient path, the road to eternity. He's telling us what our Christian lives should look like.

At the end of His sermon, Jesus says, "And every one that heareth these sayings of mine, and doeth them not, shall be likened unto a foolish man, which built his house upon the sand: and the rain descended, and the floods came, and the winds blew, and beat upon that house; and it fell: and great was the fall of it" (Matthew 7:26–27). If you want to withstand the storms of life, build on the rock—follow Jesus in obedience and live out the evidence of your new heart.

Heavenly Father, You promise us eternal life, adoption as Your children, and a home in the presence of Your glory if we can overcome in this life and throw off sin and follow You. Lord, cleanse my heart. Transform me into a pure and merciful peacemaker. Amen.

A Kingdom
for the Poor

Blessed are the poor in spirit:
for theirs is the kingdom of heaven.
MATTHEW 5:3

Pastor and author John Piper was once asked by a student if Christianity was just a crutch for people who can't make it on their own. His answer? Yes.

Crutches seem to be good for the injured or disabled who need them, but we don't like to have our weakness displayed. It grates against our pride to consider that we might not have what it takes by ourselves. That we might need support. In a 1986 sermon, John Piper said this:

The real infirmity of the world, according to Emerson, is lack of self-reliance. And so, to his dismay, along comes Christ, not with a cure for the disease, but a crutch! Christ is a stumbling block and an offense to Emerson and to all the Terry Cole-Whittaker's of our day—yes, and even to us—because it takes the disease that we hate most, namely, helplessness, and instead of curing it, makes it the doorway to heaven.

Blessed are the poor in spirit,
for theirs is the kingdom of heaven.*

Jesus beckoned to anyone who recognized their own spiritual poverty before God. It wasn't the Pharisees, who thought they had attained merit in God's eyes with their rigid religious tradition, or the nationals, who wanted to put Jesus on a throne through violence, who entered God's kingdom. It was the prostitutes, the tax collectors, the society rejects who came empty-handed before the throne of God and cried out, "God, have mercy on me, a sinner." Jesus said, "They that are whole have no need of the physician, but they that are sick: I came not to call the righteous, but sinners to repentance" (Mark 2:17).

We have no spiritual currency to purchase heaven. We have nothing to offer God, no merit in ourselves. We deserve nothing but His judgment. But in His abundant mercy, God offers His kingdom to us as a free gift, undeserved.

Jesus' intent in the Sermon on the Mount is not to send Christians into a pit of depression. Missionary to India William Carey truly was poor in spirit. He persevered for forty-one years without furlough—suffering from malaria and injury, the death of his five-year-old son, and his wife's spiral into insanity—yet translated the Bible into six languages and parts of it into twenty-nine other languages and dialects. His tombstone reveals his secret: "William Carey: A wretched, poor, and helpless worm, on Thy kind arms I fall." Poor and helpless, he threw himself into the kind and mighty arms of God.

God, I am a worthless sinner.
I place myself in Your mercy. Amen.

---

*John Piper, "Blessed Are the Poor in Spirit Who Mourn," *Desiring God*, February 2, 1986, http://www.desiringgod.org/messages/blessed-are-the-poor-in-spirit-who-mourn.

Comfort for
the Mourners

Blessed are they that mourn:
for they shall be comforted.
MATTHEW 5:4

By modern laws, David would have been a convicted murderer and a cheating husband with family problems. But God said that David was a man after His own heart (1 Samuel 13:14). And Paul reiterated this fact in the New Testament, long after David's many grave mistakes were well recorded (Acts 13:22). So how can this be? How, after committing such serious sins, was this man close to the heart of God?

When Jesus preached that the mourners would be comforted, He wasn't referring to bereavement over dead loved ones, but rather to the fact that we are all dead in our sins; we are all spiritually bankrupt before God. Jesus was talking about those who mourn their spiritual death, who sharply grieve their failure, their guilt and loss of innocence, their unworthiness and emptiness. And instead of wrapping themselves in pride and self-sufficiency, they fall to their knees in the presence of God's amazing grace. And they are comforted. "Comfort ye my people, saith your God. . .that her iniquity is pardoned" (Isaiah 40:1–2).

David knew what it meant to grieve his sins. Psalm 51 is a glimpse into his mourning heart:

Have mercy upon me, O God, according to thy
lovingkindness: according unto the multitude of thy

tender mercies blot out my transgressions. Wash me
thoroughly from mine iniquity, and cleanse me from
my sin. For I acknowledge my transgressions: and my
sin is ever before me. . . . Cast me not away from thy
presence; and take not thy holy spirit from me. . . .
For thou desirest not sacrifice; else would I give it. . .
The sacrifices of God are a broken spirit: a broken
and a contrite heart, O God, thou wilt not despise.
(vv. 1–3, 11, 16–17)

David came before God with a broken and contrite heart after committing murder and adultery. It's easy to understand his remorse for such brutal behavior, but are we moved to the point of grief for sins we consider more acceptable—anger, white lies, jealousy? Jesus placed all sin on equal ground before God: "It was said of them of old time, Thou shalt not kill. . . But I say unto you, that whosoever is angry with his brother without a cause shall be in danger of the judgment" (Matthew 5:21–22).

Jesus came to this earth to heal the brokenhearted and bind up their wounds (Psalm 147:3). He promises that those who mourn over their own wretched sinfulness will be comforted by God's free forgiveness.

Lord, I don't want to see my sin in shades of gray anymore.
Every misstep has blackened my heart. Thank You, God,
for soothing my distress with Your forgiveness. Amen.

The Meek Inherit

Blessed are the meek:
for they shall inherit the earth.
MATTHEW 5:5

How would you feel if you received a call one day from someone telling you that you were the beneficiary of a huge estate? Would you feel lucky? Over the moon? Would you feel blessed? Matthew 5:5 says, "Blessed are the meek: for they shall inherit the earth." But that doesn't seem to be the way things operate in our world. The strong and aggressive take charge with the force of their personality. They're the ones we vote most likely to succeed. Meekness isn't a character trait that we even want to identify with in today's society. Instead, we preach, "Don't be a doormat"; "You deserve this"; "Be self-made." So what is this gentle and unpretentious meekness all about, and why does it bring blessings?

To be blessed means more than mere happiness. After all, happiness is an often elusive emotion we chase, at times with limited and fickle results. The perfect sunny day at the beach can lift your flagging emotions—until the rain moves in. Happiness seems to drop in and out of our day with the unexpectedness of a pop-up shower.

But blessedness on the other hand means that joy has taken up permanent residence in us because our future is secure. John Stott wrote, "Happiness is subjective, while Jesus is making an objective judgment about these people. He is declaring not what they may feel on a particular occasion (happy), but what

God thinks of them and what they really are: they are blessed."*

You don't need to be a weak person with low self-esteem to be meek. Rather, those who are meek actually see themselves with a clarity that produces a humble attitude toward God and a gentle, compassionate love for others. While the overinflated ego of the arrogant fools them into believing they're better than they are, the meek see themselves truly and recognize the awesome grace they've been given not by their own worthiness, but through the mercy of God. First Peter 5:6 says, "Humble yourselves therefore under the mighty hand of God, that he may exalt you in due time." If we allow the Holy Spirit to foster meekness in our hearts, instead of exalting ourselves in pride that screams, "I am, and none else beside me" (Isaiah 47:10), God promises to lift us up in His time. Meekness brings the blessing of inheritance.

God, remove the pride that blinds me so that I can receive my ultimate inheritance when You return. Cultivate gentleness, kindness, and compassion in my heart. Amen.

---

*John Stott, *Reading the Sermon on the Mount with John Stott* (Downers Grove, IL: InterVarsity, 2016), 16.

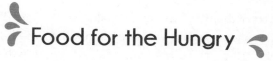

Food for the Hungry

*Blessed are they which do hunger and thirst
after righteousness: for they shall be filled.*
MATTHEW 5:6

As Christians we are called to be different from the world. Numbed to spiritual truth by prosperity, those of the world chase after more and more possessions. Success by the world's standard is weighed in dollar amounts. And if you step out of the acceptable norms of worldly behavior, some people will think you've gone out of your mind.

Mostly we hunger for power, success, money, status, comfort, relaxation—all the things we're told will make us happy. But Jesus encouraged His followers to develop a more discerning palette: "Seek ye first the kingdom of God, and his righteousness; and all these things shall be added unto you" (Matthew 6:33). He said to hunger for righteousness. And the blessing attached is that we will experience a deep fulfillment that the world can't replicate with its artificial flavoring of self-promoting behavior.

Jesus said to His disciples, "If any man will come after me, let him deny himself, and take up his cross daily, and follow me" (Luke 9:23). To these men that image meant death. The cross was an instrument of death. And Jesus was asking them to follow Him into death—the death of their old selves with their old desires—to be resurrected in new life. He says to lose yourself if you want to be found. It's a new way of living where you spend yourself not running after empty pleasures, but in service to the needy and oppressed (Isaiah 58:10).

The art of losing oneself is this: "Lord, I give You my dreams, my goals, my desires, my shortcomings. Your plans for my future are so much better than mine. I will do whatever You ask me, Jesus." The amazing thing about this process is that God has created you to be exactly who you are. He has given you unique experiences and interests. And He wants to use all of that in His plans. He wants you to do that thing you love for Him, for the growth of His kingdom.

In his book *Love Does*, Bob Goff wrote, "Every day God invites us on the same kind of adventure. It's not a trip where He sends us a rigid itinerary, He simply invites us. God asks what it is He's made us to love, what it is that captures our attention, what feeds that deep indescribable need of our souls to experience the richness of the world He made. And then, leaning over us, He whispers, 'Let's go do *that* together.' "*

God, give me a hunger for doing good in Your name.
I surrender to the adventure of kingdom living! Amen.

*Bob Goff, *Love Does: Discover a Secretly Incredible Life in an Ordinary World* (Nashville: Thomas Nelson, 2012), 129–30.

Obtaining Mercy

Blessed are the merciful:
for they shall obtain mercy.
MATTHEW 5:7

The first four beatitudes reflect our position toward God. Our poverty-stricken spirit mourns the sin we've dallied in, and we see clearly our emptiness before God. Next comes a voracious hunger for more—more of Him and His righteousness. The next three show the outward fruit of our inward attitude toward God. Our appetite for righteousness will result in mercy, purity, and peacemaking.

So what is mercy, anyway? Mercy is compassion toward others in distress that responds in practical ways to relieve that distress—even when the person in distress is an enemy.*

When the Pharisees wanted to know why Jesus was eating with tax collectors and sinners, Jesus said that the sick needed a doctor, not the healthy. Then He advised them to learn what this means: "I will have mercy, and not sacrifice: for I am not come to call the righteous, but sinners to repentance" (Matthew 9:11–13).

In Luke 10:25–37 Jesus tells a parable that sharply contrasts mercy and its opposite.

A law expert asked Jesus how he could inherit eternal life. Jesus asked him what the law said. The man replied, " 'Love the Lord your God with all your heart and with all your soul and with all your strength and with all your mind'; and, 'Love your neighbor as yourself.' " (v. 27 NIV). Jesus told him he was correct, and if he did this he would live.

But the man asked who qualified as his neighbor. So Jesus introduced him to the good Samaritan: While a man was traveling, thieves robbed and beat him, leaving him on the side of the road naked and half-dead. A priest and a Levite both saw him but crossed to the other side of the road and kept going. Then a Samaritan came and had compassion. He stopped, bandaged his wounds, put him on his donkey, and cared for him at an inn. The next day he paid the innkeeper to look after him and offered to reimburse any extra expenses when he returned.

Jesus then asked which man was a neighbor to the injured man. The law expert knew it was the merciful one. "Go, and do thou likewise," Jesus said (v. 37).

Jesus' earlier statement to the Pharisees is fleshed out in this story: God desires mercy, acting as the Samaritan did—not sacrifice, the empty religious practices of the priest and Levite whose "bondage to triviality is the curse of the unmerciful."[†]

Our God is merciful. Receive His mercy and let it compel you to likewise be merciful to others.

*God, You have given me abundant mercy
that I don't deserve. Increase my compassion
for the hurting world around me. Amen.*

---

*John Piper, "Blessed Are the Merciful," *Desiring God,* February 23, 1986,
http://www.desiringgod.org/messages/blessed-are-the-merciful.
†Ibid.

Sight for the Pure

Blessed are the pure in heart:
for they shall see God.
MATTHEW 5:8

Regardless of which side of the political fence you park your recliner on, the recent lack of government transparency has caused huge problems. This shadow world of politics allows deceit and hypocrisy to flourish because the motives of those involved never see the light of day.

You could say that both politicians and Christians at times wear masks to conceal their divided loyalties. We pretend to have it all together so no one will see our failures. We lie about our struggles, and then depression strikes because we've isolated ourselves and are now choking down Satan's lie that we are alone—that no one else could possibly understand the mess of our lives. The absence of honest sharing with our sisters in Christ leads to a lack of accountability among believers that spirals into hypocrisy, deceit, and depression.

This situation occurs when instead of a pure love for God, we suffer from a divided heart. It's not enough to look good on the outside. Jesus is concerned with the condition of our heart. The Pharisees were zealously dedicated to the law. Their standard for purity was excruciatingly high, but they had lost sight of the important matters of justice, mercy, and faith (Matthew 23:23). Jesus accused them of being whitewashed tombs, "which indeed appear beautiful outward, but are within full of dead men's bones, and of all uncleanness. Even so ye also outwardly appear righteous unto men, but within ye are full of hypocrisy and iniquity" (Matthew 23:27–28).

James wrote, "Ye adulterers and adulteresses, know ye not that the friendship of the world is enmity with God? . . . Draw nigh to God, and he will draw nigh to you. Cleanse your hands, ye sinners; and purify your hearts, ye double minded (4:4, 8). So those who are of two minds, who want both the world's pleasures and the blessings of God's kingdom, must purify their hearts in preparation for coming into God's presence. We must single-mindedly love God in order to enter His presence—where His glory is revealed (Revelation 21:23).

David prayed, "Create in me a clean heart, O God" (Psalm 51:10). We can't give ourselves a pure heart. God is the One who purifies our hearts through faith in Jesus: "And put no difference between us and them, purifying their hearts by faith" (Acts 15:9).

Let go of your worldly hangers-on—any desire that doesn't please your Father. Give Him your whole heart. Open your spiritual eyes and be wowed by the living God you see.

God, purify my heart. Remove my worldly distractions so I can see Your face. Show me the wonder of loving You with all my heart, soul, and mind. Amen.

God's Child

Blessed are the peacemakers:
for they shall be called the children of God.
MATTHEW 5:9

It is said that the *Times* of London once queried famous authors with this question: "What's wrong with the world?" And Christian writer G. K. Chesterton replied simply, "I am." The concept of sin suggests that everything is not as it should be in the world. God is perfect, and "sin is a departure from the character and will of God—a deviation from the way things ought to be. *Shalom* ("peace") in the Old Testament represents life that is well-ordered, whole, flourishing, right with God and others. By contrast, sin is anti-*shalom*. It is 'culpable shalom-breaking.' "*

The moment Adam and Eve ignored God's directions and chose their will over His, our peace with God was broken and we were separated spiritually from Him: "But your iniquities have separated between you and your God, and your sins have hid his face from you" (Isaiah 59:2). The Bible says that "all have sinned, and come short of the glory of God. . . . The wages of sin is death" (Romans 3:23; 6:23).

But God had a plan to restore peace to His rebel creations. He showed His love by sending His Son to die for sinners like us (Romans 5:8), "having made peace through the blood of his cross, by him to reconcile all things unto himself" (Colossians 1:20). And God didn't just offer us a truce—He offered us family. Through Jesus we are adopted as God's sons and daughters (Ephesians 1:5). So it seems fitting that those of us who follow in our Father's peacemaking ways should be called the children of God.

God's peace with us was costly—the life of His beloved only Son. And we shouldn't assume that the shoes of a peacemaker are always comfortable to walk in. The apostle Paul wrote, "If it be possible, as much as lieth in you, live peaceably with all men" (Romans 12:18). When someone offends us, our pride screams, "Oh no you didn't!" Blisters anyone? But peacemaking could be thought of as loving acts that extinguish the fires of animosity.

Jesus said, "Love your enemies, bless them that curse you, do good to them that hate you, and pray for them which despitefully use you, and persecute you; that ye may be the children of your Father which is in heaven" (Matthew 5:44–45). So we must be peacemakers to be children of God. And God's kids love their enemies and pray for them.

Heavenly Father, I want to be just like You when I grow up. Grant me the wisdom and humility to be a peacemaker. Amen.

---

*Robertson McQuilkin and Paul Copan, *An Introduction to Biblical Ethics*, 3rd ed. (Downers Grove, IL: InterVarsity, 2014), 98.

Blessing for the Persecuted

*Blessed are they which are persecuted for righteousness'
sake: for theirs is the kingdom of heaven. Blessed are ye,
when men shall revile you, and persecute you, and shall say
all manner of evil against you falsely, for my sake. Rejoice,
and be exceeding glad: for great is your reward in heaven:
for so persecuted they the prophets which were before you.*

MATTHEW 5:10–12

Jesus' message flows from peacemaking into persecution. Because we stand for Jesus and His righteousness, some people will insult us, spread gossip and ridicule us, or even hate us and arrange evil against us. "All that will live godly in Christ Jesus shall suffer persecution" (2 Timothy 3:12). So even if we try our hardest to be peacemakers, in this world some people will refuse to live at peace with us.

Peter said for believers not to be surprised by persecution (1 Peter 4:12), and Jesus warned that following Him puts us at odds with the world: "If the world hate you, ye know that it hated me before it hated you. If ye were of the world, the world would love his own: but because ye are not of the world, but I have chosen you out of the world, therefore the world hateth you. Remember the word that I said unto you, The servant is not greater than his lord. If they have persecuted me, they will also persecute you" (John 15:18–20).

The world rejected Jesus and murdered Him. The prophets

and disciples were ridiculed, beaten, and killed because they loved Jesus and followed His ways. We should not expect the world to accept us either. In fact, if your life doesn't look radically different from the lives of those who don't know Jesus, you should probably examine whether you are living out His commands. As Paul said, "Be not conformed to this world: but be ye transformed by the renewing of your mind" (Romans 12:2).

And instead of retaliating or running away or complaining about our circumstances, as usual believers are called to act contrary to the world's standards of behavior—Jesus says to rejoice. Rejoice that the trials you endure bring maturity to your faith. Paul said that our hardship would produce a whole harvest of fruit: endurance, good character, and hope (Romans 5:3–4). In the midst of suffering, don't be shortsighted. Rejoice—your temporary hardship for Jesus in this world brings great blessing and eternal rewards in heaven.

Jesus, transform my mind into Your way of thinking. I want to follow You even if that means suffering persecution because of my love for You. Keep my eyes focused on the eternal treasures I'm laying up in heaven instead of the temporary trials and pleasures of this world. Amen.

Back to Egypt

But he that shall endure unto the end,
the same shall be saved.
MATTHEW 24:13

Moses had promised them Canaan, so imagine the Israelites' disappointment when God led them into the desert. Actually, we don't have to imagine, for they voiced their complaints loudly: "We remember the fish, which we did eat in Egypt freely; the cucumbers, and the melons, and the leeks, and the onions, and the garlick" (Numbers 11:5). They wanted their comfort food back! It seems they would have traded freedom for bondage dripping with sauce.

A young couple moved from a house in town to a few acres in the country. One day they drove through their old town and past their former home. But when they turned onto their old street, their three-year-old daughter cried and yelled, "No, Daddy, I don't want to go back there. I want to live in our new house!" She recognized that she now had something better and vehemently refused to go back.

It's amazing that we don't always share her sentiments about our lives before we knew Jesus. But often we're so focused on our desire for what we've left behind that we forget our former slavery to it. Learning the discipline of following Jesus can be hard, and it's very easy to look back with longing when you don't keep an eternal focus. Between the alien country we were called out of and the promised land lies the desert.

The Israelites may have been slaves in Egypt, but they were

comfortable there. Here in this wilderness they didn't know what to expect. They were forced to rely on God for food, water, and even keeping their shoes together during all that tramping in the scrub. And even though God provided them manna from heaven every morning—who knew God did breakfast delivery?—their tastes ran more toward the rich foods of their past. They would need to let go of their past to move forward.

Hebrews says, "Let us lay aside every weight, and the sin which doth so easily beset us, and let us run with patience the race that is set before us, looking unto Jesus the author and finisher of our faith; who for the joy that was set before him endured the cross, despising the shame, and is set down at the right hand of the throne of God" (12:1–2). Keep your eye on Jesus and the prize of eternity. The desert is God's training ground for our faith, and He will finish His good work in you until you are "filled with the fruits of righteousness" (Philippians 1:11).

Lord, fix my eyes on You. Your promised future
is greater than my old life of slavery to sin. Amen.

Spirit of Unforgiveness

Forbearing one another, and forgiving one another, if any man have a quarrel against any: even as Christ forgave you, so also do ye.
COLOSSIANS 3:13

Outside of love, one of Jesus' greatest commands is that we forgive. His biggest contention with the Pharisees was that they didn't understand God's love and were unmerciful. He called them things like whitewashed tombs that were dead inside and blind guides who strained out gnats but had swallowed a camel because they were so tied up by inconsequential trivialities that they had missed the finer points of the law: "To do justly, and to love mercy, and to walk humbly with thy God" (Matthew 23:23–24; Micah 6:8). They loved their pride most of all—at the expense of justice, mercy, and humility.

Without forgiveness we can't love. If we can't forgive, we will destroy ourselves through resentment and anger that will fester into hatred or self-loathing. It's really hard to love when you have hatred in your heart. We're not called to show mercy just in the big stuff—like abuse or murder. We're called to forgive *all* things, and that means the small things too. Sometimes we don't see the danger here because it seems inconsequential to be offended by someone's words or actions.

Have you ever noticed that the tiniest splinter can cause so much pain? The wound can fester and swell until all you can think about is the pain from that sliver. Little girls hate to have splinters pulled out. We bribe them with candy, but they still scream like banshees. We calmly explain, "Honey, you can't leave this here. I know it seems little, but if we don't pull it out, it will get infected." And infection can spread and poison your whole body. Infection can lead to death.

Unforgiveness is like that tiny splinter. It can poison your whole attitude and mind with bitterness. This is important for women to grasp because we're sensitive. Our feelings get hurt and we're easily offended, especially if we feel slighted or left out; or heaven forbid that someone says something less than flattering about our kids, our home, or our clothes.

Examine your reactions to people. Have you been overly sensitive to the things people say and do? Are you looking for an offense in every interaction? The first step is admitting that you have harbored offense against others in your heart.

Father, I'm so glad that I'm created in Your image. Help me to remember that my worth comes from You and only Your opinion matters. Open my spiritual eyes and show me where I have been holding grudges and soaking in self-pity. Show me the way to forgiveness. Amen.

Amazing Love

I have loved thee with an everlasting love:
therefore with lovingkindness have I drawn thee.
JEREMIAH 31:3

Love. Have you tread upon the violent waters of this raw emotion? Bliss, despair, anger, joy, sadness, pain, happiness, lust, fear—in today's culture we often roll a payload of volatile emotions into a package with nuclear potential and brand it as love.

Some of you have been wounded by people you thought loved you, who then inflicted deep pain through selfish or violent acts. You have known inconstant love, where one day you were wanted and the next the feeling had withered—they'd "fallen out of love" with you. Some of you have been victims of faithless love or conditional love or selfish love or controlling love.

But know this truth, beloved daughter of God's heart: none of those experiences is love. And God's love doesn't look like any of those things. His love is proved in what He does: "Herein is love, not that we loved God, but that he loved us, and sent his Son to be the propitiation for our sins" (1 John 4:10). The Greek word for God's love is *agape*. It means that God chooses to love us with a sacrificial love so great that He would die to *do* what is best for us, even when we don't like it. And He would do that without expecting anything in return. God-love is not a fickle emotion. It's action.

We say that love is a lot of things in this world, but 1 Corinthians unveils its true face. Love is patient and kind. It is never envious or proud. It is never selfish and doesn't dishonor others.

144

It is not easily angered and doesn't keep a record of wrongs. Love rejoices in the truth. It always protects, always trusts, always hopes, always perseveres. Love never fails (13:4–8). My friend, God loves you. Let your thoughts steep in that simple knowledge for a few moments.

Paul prayed this for Jesus' followers: "That Christ may dwell in your hearts by faith; that ye, being rooted and grounded in love, may be able to comprehend with all saints what is the breadth, and length, and depth, and height; and to know the love of Christ, which passeth knowledge, that ye might be filled with all the fulness of God" (Ephesians 3:17–19). God's love is infinite. We aren't capable of *agape* in ourselves, but the Holy Spirit fills our hearts with God's incomprehensible—great and amazing—love. "Beloved, if God so loved us, we ought also to love one another" (1 John 4:11).

God, I can hardly believe that You would love me like that.
That You would come down from glory and die just for me.
Pour Your love into my heart so I can love too. Amen.

Incomprehensible

God thundereth marvellously with his voice;
great things doeth he, which we cannot comprehend.
JOB 37:5

The little girl stared hard, but nothing changed. She squinted at the tiny birds covering the page, tilting her head to one side and then the other. Nothing happened. It still looked like tiny white birds stacked in flat rows. "I can't see it," she said. "Here, look at it this way." Her mother held the book just off the end of her nose and slowly backed it away from her face. And suddenly a 3-D image of birds in flight snapped into focus and seemed to hover over the page. She was amazed that a picture could hide something like that. Optical illusions have a way of masking the bigger picture until we gain the right perspective. But even seeing it in front of us doesn't explain how it's done.

Isn't that what happens to our concept of God sometimes? We think we know all about Him and have a pretty good idea about what He's capable of—then suddenly through nature or hardship or joy, He reveals more of Himself to us, and we realize that our imagination cannot contain Him. Our human perspective limits our expectations of Him—but He is wilder than we thought. Much like 85 percent of an iceberg is submerged beneath frigid waters, our minds comprehend precious little of the true greatness of God.

In his book *The Attributes of God*, A. W. Tozer wrote, "God is infinite! That's the hardest thought I will ask you to grasp. You cannot understand what infinite means, but don't let it bother you—I don't understand it and I'm trying to explain it! . . . We mean by infinite that God knows no limits, no bounds and no end. What God is, He is without boundaries."*

So everything we know about the character and abilities of God—His power, knowledge, presence, goodness, justice, mercy, grace, perfection, and holiness—are all without border or limit. That's huge!

There is no other like Him. He is the One and Only: "Beside me there is no God" (Isaiah 44:6). And He is eternal: "I am Alpha and Omega, the beginning and the ending, saith the Lord, which is, and which was, and which is to come, the Almighty. . . . I am. . .the first and the last" (Revelation 1:8; 22:13).

Find comfort in the awesome greatness of your God. And consider: *Is my concept of God too small for the mighty God I serve? How would seeing Him in a bigger way change my life?*

God, reveal more of Your greatness to me.
Strip away the limits I have forced on You. Amen.

---

*A. W. Tozer, *The Attributes of God* (Chicago: WingSpread, 1997), 4.

Diamonds

*The sufferings of this present time are not worthy to be
compared with the glory which shall be revealed in us.*
ROMANS 8:18

What if we accepted hard things in our lives as blessings instead of burdens? How radically that would transform our thinking and our attitudes. Suddenly troubles are no longer a stumbling block to our faith but an opportunity for spiritual growth—no longer a punishment but a gift. Mother Teresa said, "I never call difficulties 'problems.' I always say, 'gift of God,' because it is always much easier to take a gift than to take a problem."*

So often we doubt God's love for us in the face of hardship, question His ways, and feel sorry for ourselves. We listen to Satan's whisper that God doesn't really care about the mundane moments in our insignificant lives. But scripture says just the opposite—that God saw us in the womb, and He knew what each and every day of our lives would hold before we were born (Psalm 139:15–16).

My friend, when you encounter something that's hard to handle, don't go down the path of self-pity. Instead, "count it all joy" because God is working to complete you, to make you "perfect and entire, wanting nothing" (James 1:2–4). The God who forms worlds has promised that He is at work in you: "He which hath begun a good work in you will perform it until the day of Jesus Christ" (Philippians 1:6). If you can bring yourself to surrender, imagine what He could do.

Too often we're blinded by Satan's lie that if God truly loved us He would take away all of our trials and fill our days with comfort and ease. But the truth is that God is less concerned with ridding us of all our burdens than with who we become because of them. He loves us enough to use tough love, to gift us with the opportunity to grow into something better, stronger, and deeper than we were before. "For our light affliction, which is but for a moment, worketh for us a far more exceeding and eternal weight of glory; while we look not at the things which are seen, but at the things which are not seen: for the things which are seen are temporal; but the things which are not seen are eternal" (2 Corinthians 4:17–18). The key to counting hard things as joy is changing your focus from the present to the eternal.

When the pressure of life is on, ask God to change *you* instead of your circumstances, and trust Him to work "an eternal weight of glory" in you.

God, open my eyes to the beauty on the other side of my difficulties. Change me. Amen.

*Mother Teresa, *Where There Is Love, There Is God*, ed. Brian Kolodiejchuk (New York: Doubleday Religion, 2010), 169.

My Defender

He ever liveth to make intercession for them.
HEBREWS 7:25

Many Christians harshly discount their worth: "I'm useless, a no-good failure." We believe Satan's lies that we've been benched by inadequacy and mistakes. But don't buy everything you hear. Satan is known as "the accuser of our brethren. . .which accused them before our God day and night" (Revelation 12:10). Learn to recognize his hateful indictments against you so you won't be robbed of the peace we have through Christ.

In his book *The Bondage Breaker*, Neil T. Anderson writes about one Christian's defeat: "My old feelings that life isn't worth the trouble keep coming back. I'm scared, lonely, confused, and very desperate. I know deep down that God can overcome this, but I can't get past this block. . . . I'm stopped dead in my tracks by those voices and a force so strong I can't continue. I'm so close to giving in to those voices that I almost can't fight them anymore. I just want some peace."*

We don't have to listen to Satan's accusations. He may be reading the charges against you, my friend, but God sits on His bench as judge. In Zechariah chapter 3 the prophet has a vision of Satan's courtroom defeat: "He shewed me Joshua the high priest standing before the angel of the LORD, and Satan standing at his right hand to resist him. And the LORD said unto Satan, The LORD rebuke thee, O Satan; even the LORD that hath chosen Jerusalem rebuke thee: is not this a brand plucked out of the fire? Now Joshua was clothed with filthy garments, and stood before the angel" (vv. 1–3).

"Look at those filthy rags!" Satan says, "Give him death!" Daily Satan points out our mess-ups to God. But God puts Satan's accusations in their place: "You will not sentence my people. I have rescued them from the fire of judgment." And Jesus, our defense attorney, stands on our behalf: "These charges are baseless. My client has been justified through my death and resurrection" (see Romans 8:33–34). Satan may fill your mind with thoughts of your unworthiness, but remind him that his defeat is already final. You are a daughter of God through Jesus.

God says, "Take away the filthy garments from him. . . . I have caused thine iniquity to pass from thee, and I will clothe thee with change of raiment" (Zechariah 3:4). You no longer stand before God in filthy rags of sin; instead, you're clothed in the righteousness of Christ.

Thank You, Jesus, for standing with me in the face of Satan's accusations. I am not worthless to You. I am Your righteous daughter. Amen.

---

*Neil T. Anderson, *The Bondage Breaker* (Eugene, OR: Harvest House, 1993), 142.

Moving Up

Dearly beloved, I beseech you as strangers and pilgrims,
abstain from fleshly lusts, which war against the soul.
1 PETER 2:11

> *Just beyond where the shadows are falling*
> *Is a bright, summer land, ever fair.**

Who doesn't love vacations—seeing amazing new places, relaxing and unloading our stress? But enjoyable as they are, while we're there we rarely fully unpack. We often don't use the dresser drawers or take our toiletries out of our travel bags. We definitely don't hang pictures or buy new rugs, because we know our visit is temporary.

> Have you ever thought about eternity?
> Forever.
> On and on and on and on.

Ten thousand years can pass and there's still more. Never-ending life. It's like staring out over the ocean on a hazy day when the water smudges into the horizon and appears to extend unendingly. When we get to that place, this world will seem like a blink.

So why do we allow eternally inconsequential things to hold so much weight in our minds? Why do our troubles and desires wreck us? The apostle Peter said that if we continually increase our faith, goodness, knowledge, self-control, perseverance, godliness, kindness, and love, we will be received "abundantly into the everlasting kingdom of our Lord and Saviour Jesus Christ" (2 Peter 1:1–11). He doesn't say that the person with the most stuff wins.

Corrie ten Boom and her family saved the lives of approximately eight hundred Jews during the Nazi Holocaust and were sent to a concentration camp in 1944. She once said, "Hold everything in your hands lightly; otherwise it hurts when God pries your fingers open." In other words, don't unpack your suitcase here. Don't put your hope in your own dream—the perfect husband, kids, house, and job. Instead, rest these blessings on open palms.

Each of us is faced with the choice between self or God's kingdom. We must learn to experience the double vision of spiritual sight. We see the world and its giant heap of stuff, but something different flickers before our spiritual eyes like a shimmer of heat in the atmosphere—golden streets and a place where love really did conquer all. Allow this glimpse of glory to drive you to work in God's kingdom with renewed energy and purpose—to be patient when your flesh cries out in frustration, to serve joyfully in love in spite of your wilting strength.

Our inheritance is kept for us in heaven, unspoiled. Don't get too comfortable here. Remember what you're building. Glory awaits!

❧

Heavenly Father, my life here can seem more real than Your kingdom; keep my spiritual vision alive. Amen.

---

*Hymn lyrics from "Beyond the Shadows," by Charles W. Naylor, 1907.

Why?

*Therefore have I uttered that I understood not;
things too wonderful for me, which I knew not.*
JOB 42:3

Sometimes we just want answers. We want to understand the workings of God and know exactly what the big picture is. We need assurance that all the hard things and struggles, our joys, our choices—they all matter. We want to ask why and have everything explained in a way that satisfies both our curiosity and sense of fairness. Like three-year-olds, we want everything to add up equally.

But we know that, painfully limited by the inexperience of youth, three-year-olds are difficult to reason with. And it is purely our arrogance and pride that demand an explanation from God and expect that our fragile minds could comprehend the thoughts of the eternal God: "Shall the clay say to him that fashioneth it, What makest thou?" (Isaiah 45:9).

Job loved God, but he lost everything. Then his unhelpful friends accused him of sin (11:14–15) and his peach of a wife told him to curse God and die (2:9). In the end, God didn't answer Job's *why*. Instead, He put a series of questions to Job and his friends and dared them to answer:

Where wast thou when I laid the foundations of the earth? declare, if thou hast understanding. . . . Have the gates of death been opened unto thee? . . . Hast thou perceived the breadth of the earth? declare

154

if thou knowest it all. Where is the way where light dwelleth? and as for darkness, where is the place thereof. . . ? . . . Knowest thou it, because thou wast then born? or because the number of thy days is great? (Job 38:4, 17–19, 21)

God doesn't have to explain Himself to us or love us, but He does. He wants us to know His good character, and He loves each one of us as if we were His only love. As Paul reminds us, "For now we see through a glass, darkly; but then face to face: now I know in part; but then shall I know even as also I am known" (1 Corinthians 13:12). To know and be known—what a comforting promise!

When Jesus returns for us, we will understand God's work here. Because He is sovereign, He can protect us from hidden dangers we didn't know to look for, and bring us closer to Him through circumstances we don't understand. He's weaving His plan through our lives, telling His story. And His plot is tight. Can you humble your pride before Him and admit that He is greater than you?

God, Your ways are not mine. I don't always understand what You're setting in motion. You plot the course in millennia while I count days. I trust my life to Your plan. Amen.

Living Sacrifice

*Present your bodies a living sacrifice, holy,
acceptable unto God, which is your reasonable service.*
ROMANS 12:1

Do we present ourselves to the Lord as living sacrifices? Do we actually know what this looks like? In the Old Testament, the sacrifice died. What part of you needs to die in order for you to serve Christ? Followers of Jesus daily experience death and life—the death of self and sin and new life in Jesus. Yet we all harbor the self-serving desire to do whatever we want. Becoming a living sacrifice means repeatedly asking, "Am I going to go my own way, or am I going to obey God?"

The truest form of love is sacrifice. Words are cheap. They're just vapor until we put the substance of action behind them. When we deny our flesh because it is holy and acceptable to God, we show Him that we love Him more than anything—we love His Word more than that TV show we were going to watch, we love His law more than the satisfaction we get from retaliating when someone hurts us.

When our husbands, kids, and friends see us sacrificing ourselves for them, they experience the deep love of Jesus. What greater witness to Jesus' amazing love and tremendous sacrifice can there be? If your mind is in unity with the Spirit, you will discover unspeakable joy in fulfilling Paul's plea to the Roman churches: "I beseech you therefore, brethren, by the mercies of God, that ye present your bodies a living sacrifice, holy, acceptable unto God, which is your reasonable service" (Romans 12:1).

And how do we know what is holy and acceptable to God? Verse 2 explains: "Be not conformed to this world: but be ye transformed by the renewing of your mind, that ye may prove what is that good, and acceptable, and perfect, will of God."

You need to get a new mind, friend! Let Jesus shift and change your mind-set so you will know how to do God's will. Allow His scouring Word to cleanse your mind of worldly philosophy and replace it with His holy and perfect precepts, given out of love for your good. Living according to God's Word leads ultimately to your best life!

The things that bring you joy and satisfaction transform when your thinking centers on God and the leathered flesh of your toughened heart is softened by the moisturizing oil of His love. Presenting your body as a living sacrifice will become your goal, and pleasing your Father will become your greatest joy!

God, take my life and use it for Your glory. Take my mind and transform it. Make every action I take a holy and acceptable offering to You that brings a smile to Your face, Father. In Jesus' name, amen.

Fully Rely on God

I am the living bread which came down from heaven.
JOHN 6:51

THREE EX-BILLIONAIRES SEE FORTUNES WIPED OUT IN STOCK ROUT. This recent headline reminds us of how careful we must be to put our hope in God and not in the wealth of this world. Fortunes here are sometimes made and lost in a blink, and our self-sufficiency can hinder our dependence on God.

In the wilderness, God wanted to teach the Israelites that He supplied all their needs. The learning curve of the desert classroom is steep. And God humbled them by making them helpless. He took them to a desolate place where they had to rely on His provision. And then He proved Himself trustworthy by giving them everything they ever needed.

Before the Israelites crossed the Jordan into Canaan, Moses gave them this warning not to forget the lessons of the desert:

Remember all the way which the LORD thy God led thee these forty years in the wilderness. . . And he humbled thee, and suffered thee to hunger, and fed thee with manna. . .that he might make thee know that man doth not live by bread only, but by every word that proceedeth out of the mouth of the LORD. . . . Lest when thou hast eaten and art full, and hast built goodly houses, and dwelt therein. . .then thine heart be lifted up, and thou forget the LORD thy God, which brought thee forth out of the land of Egypt, from the house of bondage; who led thee through that great and terrible wilderness, wherein were fiery serpents, and scorpions. . .who brought thee forth water out of the rock of flint. . .and thou say in thine heart, My power and the might of mine hand hath gotten me this wealth. But thou shalt remember the LORD thy God: for it is he that giveth thee power to get wealth, that he may establish his covenant which he sware unto thy fathers. (Deuteronomy 8:2–3, 12, 14–15, 17–18)

Jesus said it was easier for a camel to go through the eye of a needle than for a rich man to enter the kingdom of heaven (Mark 10:25). It's not that a rich person can't enter the kingdom; it's just harder to see our need for God when we have everything. The danger of wealth is that it can make us proud. Living the high life can feel like the good life, but God wants us to understand that real living and fulfillment come from relying completely on Him and living by every word that comes from Him. The things of this world will never satisfy our deepest longings.

God, You supply all of my needs. Satisfy my soul as I feast on the bread of Your Word. Amen.

Poured-Out Love

*For God so loved the world, that he gave his
only begotten Son, that whosoever believeth in
him should not perish, but have everlasting life.*

JOHN 3:16

C. S. Lewis wrote in his book *The Four Loves* that. . .

> *to love at all is to be vulnerable. Love anything, and
> your heart will certainly be wrung and possibly be
> broken. If you want to make sure of keeping it intact,
> you must give your heart to no one, not even to an
> animal. Wrap it carefully round with hobbies and
> little luxuries; avoid all entanglements; lock it up safe
> in the casket—safe, dark, motionless, airless—it will
> change. It will not be broken; it will become unbreak-
> able, impenetrable, irredeemable. The alternative to
> tragedy is damnation. The only place outside Heaven
> where you can be perfectly safe from all the dangers
> and perturbations of love is Hell.**

Too often we don't love one another because we're afraid
to be vulnerable. We're afraid to expose ourselves and fear the
cost—because love can hurt. Whether it is the pain of a broken
relationship or the pain of sacrifice, loving anything will cost you.
Jesus paid painfully to love us. He "being in the form of God,
thought it not robbery to be equal with God: but made himself
of no reputation, and took upon him the form of a servant, and
was made in the likeness of men: and being found in fashion

as a man, he humbled himself, and became obedient unto death, even the death of the cross" (Philippians 2:6–8). Jesus definitely was not trading up when He wrapped Himself in rags of humanity to demonstrate the depths of God's love for us.

Sacrifice isn't thought of very highly today. We're all about comfort, entertainment, and pleasure. We are often unwilling to inconvenience ourselves even momentarily for one another. So the thought of pouring out our lives in love seems ludicrous. But that's exactly what Jesus did. He emptied Himself and became nothing. He gave up glory to love us. It's impossible to imagine a more vulnerable position than being stripped and beaten and hung high on a cross for everyone to gawk as your body fails you in death.

If you've ever doubted God's love for you, know that love isn't just a feeling He entertains at His whim, it is the very fiber of His being. It's who He is. He can't do other than love us because "God is love" (1 John 4:8). And He commands us to love as He does (John 15:12). When was the last time you emptied yourself to love another?

God, Your love humbles and amazes me. May Your Spirit in me give me strength to love until it hurts, for "when I am weak, then am I strong" (2 Corinthians 12:10). Amen.

---

*C. S. Lewis, *The Four Loves* (San Diego, CA: Harvest Books, 1971), 121.

Treasured Possession

If ye will obey my voice indeed,
and keep my covenant, then ye shall be a
peculiar treasure unto me above all people.
EXODUS 19:5

A man's wife pointed out that their back door rubbed the floor slightly when opened. But he was late for work, and in spite of noting the resistance as it brushed over the hardwood floor, he didn't stop to fix it. Months went by, and the man could never fit the door repair into his plans. Over time the door scraped a deep groove into the hardwood floor. When he finally looked at the door, the man discovered a loose hinge, a five-minute fix. But since he had ignored the problem for so long, he now had to face the expensive and time-consuming task of replacing the wood floor in the whole entryway.

Unfortunately, the moment we're saved doesn't deliver us into instant glowing perfection, as much as we wish it did. But it's not a magic eraser for a lifetime of bad habits and poor attitudes. This Christian life is a journey of learning to walk with God—both in obedience to God's Word and in the Spirit's power.

Sometimes we get a little out of line—maybe we get a little too worked up about something trivial, or we indulge our appetite with that extra scoop of ice cream, or we allow longing to turn into jealousy. Sin can sneak into our lives in small ways and grow. Most people don't just get out of bed one day and go into a raging tirade at their kids or drink themselves into a stupor with no prior offenses. The real problem comes when we ignore that first small act of sin—that first self-serving choice.

The apostle Paul wrote that we must take our thoughts captive and bring them into obedience to Christ (2 Corinthians 10:5). We don't have to be at the mercy of our thoughts because "we all had our conversation in times past in the lusts of our flesh, fulfilling the desires of the flesh and of the mind. . . But God, who is rich in mercy, for his great love wherewith he loved us. . .hath quickened us together with Christ" (Ephesians 2:3–5).

It's freeing to know that we can choose to obey; we can choose life with Christ over death in sin. Today, don't let negative attitudes and wrong actions spiral out of control. Extinguish those thoughts the moment they spring to life in your mind. Choose joy. Choose peace. Choose kindness and goodness, patience and love. Choose life!

Father, help me to correct small sins before they become big issues. Reveal to me areas of sin in my life, and bring me into obedience to Your Word. Make me Your treasure. Amen.

Spirit of Forgiveness

Let all bitterness, and wrath, and anger, and clamour, and evil speaking, be put away from you, with all malice: and be ye kind one to another, tenderhearted, forgiving one another, even as God for Christ's sake hath forgiven you.
EPHESIANS 4:31–32

Why do my feelings get hurt so easily? Why am I so sensitive all the time? To conquer a spirit of unforgiveness, we have to root out the hard feelings, resentment, bitterness, anger, and hurt in our lives. Don't shove those things into a corner. Bring all those harmful emotions into the light of Jesus. Come to "the Father of mercies, and the God of all comfort; who comforteth us in all our tribulation" (2 Corinthians 1:3–4). He's big enough to contain your emotions, and if you ask Him, He will help you to clearly see the way through.

Forgiveness is a choice. Proverbs says, "The discretion of a man deferreth his anger; and it is his glory to pass over a transgression" (19:11). So we can choose to say, "I refuse to take offense." Refusing to take offense doesn't mean we excuse wrong actions; it means that we don't obsess over how we've been hurt and play others' nasty words and actions on a loop in our minds. This only feeds into our own anger and resentment.

Instead, try listening without insult. Find out what is driving others' words or actions. Ask yourself objectively, *Is what they're saying true? Do I need improvement in this area? Or is there some deep root of pain in their life that is causing them to lash out at others?* Everyone benefits if you choose not to be offended. You won't be pouting over a slight and may even learn a lesson God wants to teach you. And you don't risk inflicting more pain on an already hurting soul.

Jesus said, "Blessed are the merciful: for they shall obtain mercy" (Matthew 5:7). He was talking to His followers about what our Christian walk should look like—that our actions prove our faith. If we have admitted our own sin and need for forgiveness and accepted God's gift of forgiveness, then we will also be able to forgive others. So being merciful is evidence that God's mercy has been planted in us and we are indeed children of God.

Ask God for your spiritual eyes to be opened to the pain of others, and overlooking their offenses will seem like less of a burden.

Jesus, You have forgiven me much, so I can in turn forgive much. You comfort me when I have been slighted. Give me eyes to see where others are hurting. And give me clarity to recognize when I am wrong. Amen.

Let Peace Reign

Let the peace of God rule in your hearts.
COLOSSIANS 3:15

A group of kids form a line and join hands to play crack the whip. The little boy on one end stands fixed while the others run in a circle around him like a wheel spoke, struggling to keep the line straight. And the unfortunate kid on the whip's tail sprints like a wild child to stay with the group.

This world isn't exactly tranquil. All we have to do is click on the news to be overloaded with floods, terrorist attacks, fraud scandals, political unrest, school shootings, and the refugee crisis—reporters paint a portrait of the world gone mad. And that's not to mention the rising anxiety levels and overbooked schedules that stampede through our everyday lives.

Becoming a Christian doesn't guarantee nothing bad will ever brush against your life again. In fact, coming to know Jesus may gain you new enemies. Satan will notice that you now follow Jesus. He wasn't concerned about you when you were living as the world lives, but now that you belong to Jesus, he will actively target you. In his book *The Journey*, Billy Graham wrote, "Don't think of Satan as a harmless cartoon character with a red suit and a pitchfork. He is very clever and powerful, and his unchanging purpose is to defeat God's plans at every turn—including His plans for your life."*

So we can expect trouble as long as we're walking around in this battle zone called Earth, but Jesus gives us the perfect tool to use against calamity—His peace. Jesus said, "These things I have spoken unto you, that in me ye might have peace. In the world ye shall have tribulation: but be of good cheer; I have overcome the world" (John 16:33). If we make Jesus the center of our lives, much like the center child in crack the whip, we will possess inner calmness, security, and peace, even as the world runs crazily around us.

If your journey in life has been spent grasping for fulfillment you can't seem to reach, maybe you're running after pleasure, comfort, excitement, or success instead of standing beside Jesus. Jesus said, "Peace I leave with you, my peace I give unto you: not as the world giveth, give I unto you. Let not your heart be troubled, neither let it be afraid" (John 14:27). The farther away from Jesus you get, the faster you run after anything that might fill your desires. What empty promise of satisfaction are you chasing?

Jesus, anxiety and worry war with Your peace in my heart. Help me to give peace the rule of my heart and mind. Amen.

*Billy Graham, *The Journey: How to Live by Faith in an Uncertain World* (Nashville: Thomas Nelson, 2006), 35.

God's Goodness

*Why callest thou me good? there is
none good but one, that is, God.*
MARK 10:18

The prince-turned-Beast, Mr. Darcy, and Mr. Rochester—some of the most real and believable fictional characters have mixed motives—noble yet sprinkled with failures, shortcomings, and self-serving inclinations too. They don't always win the congeniality contest, but we love them in spite of it—because we can relate. Because in truth, we're all a bit shaded.

But sometimes we imagine that God has these same weaknesses of character that unite us as humans. But it's important that we ask ourselves, *What is God like?* and compare our preconceived ideas of His character with the truth of scripture. Just as first impressions are not always correct, it's possible to have the wrong impression of God—especially if you don't know Him very well.

God is good—*always* good and *only* good. No gray motives darken the piercing brilliance of His character. The apostle John wrote, "God is light, and in him is no darkness at all" (1 John 1:5). Have you ever woken up on the wrong side of the bed? Summiting Mount Everest might be more within your grasp than producing pleasant conversation—especially if you haven't yet downed at least two-thirds of your daily caffeine intake. But God isn't a coffee addict. He doesn't require an artificial jump start to His morning personality.

Since God is perfect and infinite, so is His goodness. His

perfection means that He is always perfectly good. "O taste and see that the LORD is good" (Psalm 34:8). And because He is infinite, His goodness is without limits. Think about that. God is *all* that is good. If there was something good that was outside of God, then He wouldn't be perfectly or infinitely good! There's no evil bend to His mind, no selfish motives driving His actions. He works from the infinite well of His good heart.

So what does it mean to be *good*? The word used here is defined as "pleasant, delightful, cheerful, kind, correct, and righteous." We know about God's moral goodness, His righteousness, but do we also believe the first part of this description—that God is also pleasant and cheerful and kind? You might believe this of your white-haired granny who bakes chocolate chip cookies every time you visit, but know this: God's goodness makes Him approachable and benevolent. "How excellent is thy lovingkindness, O God!" (Psalm 36:7).

Do you sometimes believe God is picking on you? Or do you trust that God always acts out of kindness and goodness?

God, thank You for the good gifts You give—
that out of Your infinite goodness You both
created us and redeemed us through Jesus. Amen.

Big Faith

*Now the God of hope fill you with all joy and
peace in believing, that ye may abound in
hope, through the power of the Holy Ghost.*
ROMANS 15:13

In her recent book *Your Dream. God's Plan.*, Tiffany Smiling tells of a courageous woman of faith: Yvrose and her thirty-four adopted children live in five small sheet-metal buildings near the coast in Haiti. In the face of approaching Hurricane Matthew, when everyone was running for cover, Yvrose gathered all her children in one room and gave an incredible command: sing praises to the Lord. Then she ran out into the downpour to help others. " 'I told them to sing,' she explained to me. 'What else could we do but praise the God who was going to save us from the storm?' What else, indeed."*

God wanted the Israelites to wait in faith instead of fear for Him to move on their behalf. But unlike Yvrose, with their backs to the Red Sea the Israelites started to panic when Pharaoh's army advanced on their vulnerable position: "Weren't there enough graves in Egypt? Did you bring us here to die?" they yelled at Moses. But Moses trusted in the future that God had already promised them. "Fear ye not, stand still, and see the salvation of the LORD, which he will shew to you to day: for the Egyptians whom ye have seen to day, ye shall see them again no more for ever. The LORD shall fight for you, and ye shall hold your peace" (Exodus 14:13–14).

Be still. Don't be afraid. Remember God's promises to you

and stand firm in His loving faithfulness. God will fight for you! Moses' words to the Israelites hold all the hope of a mighty and loving God who is able to do great things—while we gape in slack-jawed amazement.

And that isn't the only time God proved His reliability. Water tends to be a little scarce in the desert. And the Israelites were getting thirsty. Once again they freaked out instead of trusting God. They were about to stone Moses (temporary insanity, maybe?) when God told him to strike the rock at Horeb. And water flowed from solid rock for His people. Next the Israelites ran afoul of some hostiles. The Amalekites were a plundering tribe of warriors who enjoyed killing. But God defeated them with a ragtag bunch of former slaves.

We, like the Israelites, are saved through God's action, not our own. Jesus calms our storms with the words "Be still!" In the face of such proof, as He asked the disciples, "Do you still have no faith?"

God, You have proven Your faithfulness.
Increase my faith! Amen.

---

*Tiffany Smiling with Margot Starbuck, *Your Dream. God's Plan.* (Uhrichsville, OH: Barbour, 2017).

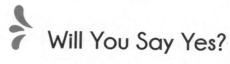

Will You Say Yes?

Now ye are the body of Christ,
and members in particular.
1 CORINTHIANS 12:27

A story is told of a woman whose husband was away at war. He called his wife from the airport. "Honey, I'm coming home, but I have a favor to ask. I have a friend I'd like to bring home with me."

"Sure," she said. "I'd love to meet him."

"There's something you should know, Liz," the man said. "He was hurt bad in the fighting. He stepped on a land mine and lost an arm and a leg. He has nowhere else to go, and I want him to come live with us."

"Oh honey, maybe we can help him find somewhere to live."

"No, Liz. I want him to live with us." The line was silent for a moment.

"John, have you thought about this? That would be such a huge burden. You've been gone so long, and we have our own lives to live. I don't think we should move him in with us."

Her husband hung up; his flight was boarding. Hours later she received a call from the police. Her husband had died after falling from a building. The police believed it was suicide.

Shocked and grief-stricken, she drove to the city morgue to identify the body. It was her John, but to her horror, she discovered he had only one arm and one leg.

At the Last Supper, Jesus' final meal with His disciples before He died, He warned them that they would disown Him and be scattered that night (Matthew 26:31–34). How often do we disown Jesus with our actions by refusing to do His work, by refusing to be His hands and feet in this broken, hurting world? God has a unique plan for each one of us—kingdom work He has equipped us to do.

Examine your heart, beloved. Are you saying no to God when He asks for your help? Do the tasks you undertake each day have any eternal value, or have you been caught in a cycle of self-focused living? The lonely are in despair; orphans are starving for not only food, but love; people are walking in the darkness. Will they die because you've said no? "Ye are the light of the world. A city that is set on an hill cannot be hid. Neither do men light a candle, and put it under a bushel, but on a candlestick; and it giveth light unto all that are in the house. Let your light so shine before men, that they may see your good works, and glorify your Father which is in heaven" (Matthew 5:14–16).

God, make me willing. I don't want to
deny You through a self-focused life. Amen.

You Can Do It!

And what is the exceeding greatness of his power to us-ward who believe, according to the working of his mighty power, which he wrought in Christ, when he raised him from the dead, and set him at his own right hand in the heavenly places, far above all principality, and power, and might, and dominion, and every name that is named, not only in this world, but also in that which is to come.

EPHESIANS 1:19–21

Palms scraped from your latest stumble, you've encountered tough terrain along your trek with Jesus—frightening places where the ominous mountains of trial loom over the distant mist. You grabbed His hand and fortified yourself with scripture. And when the road under your feet tilted upward and the cliffs above you rose, jagged and sharp, you whispered to yourself, "*I can't. I can't do this! It's too hard. It's too painful. It's just too much!*" Yep, you scrambled out of there fast! You didn't spare a backward glance until that peak was once again at a safe distance.

Raise your hand with me if you've ever doubted your Wonder Woman for Jesus capabilities. If you've prayed for His will and then run screaming from the revelation staring back at you. If you've slapped the covers of your Bible back together after a shocking dip in God's Word and thought, *What is that all about, God?* We've conditioned and trained, but in the moment of truth our efforts can still be subverted on the battleground of our mind before we set even one foot into the first toehold of our climb.

Focusing on your own strength will always land you on your backside, because the truth is we *can't* do this Christian life on our own. We can't understand God's ways. We can't overcome sin. We can't fulfill His plan for our lives by ourselves. You might be asking, *Then why am I even trying?* Because you're not alone! Women of strength and independence, when will we admit that we need Him?

He might set us on hard roads, but we have His supernatural source of power fueling us—and this promise from the God incapable of lies: "I can do all things through Christ which strengtheneth me" (Philippians 4:13). Those hills might tower dangerously high, but He can flatten them under your feet—or maybe you prefer rocket boots. Our God is able, so we don't have to be! "The things which are impossible with men are possible with God" (Luke 18:27). You can do it, friend. When God calls, He also equips!

Lord Jesus, the power to do Your will flows from You.
Equip me for the work You have planned.
Let's face that mountain again. Together. Amen.

Escape Plan

Humble yourselves in the sight of the Lord,
and he shall lift you up.
JAMES 4:10

A nine-month-old baby boy cracks a dimpled grin at the camera. His parents are eager to capture every moment of their outing in photos. A scant few feet behind the happy, clueless toddler, a lioness crouches, paw raised in a blurred swipe. BABY OBLIVIOUS TO LION TRYING TO ATTACK HIM AT ZOO the headline reads. Thankfully the child had safaried to a glass enclosure and not the Sahara!

Unfortunately, some believers are as painfully unaware of their precarious positions of faith as this carefree baby, except they're naked to attack—no laminated layers of tempered glass to protect them. And like that lioness, our enemy bats at our vulnerable places with the razor-tipped claws of temptation.

The Corinthian Christians had been "enriched by [Christ Jesus], in all utterance, and in all knowledge" (1 Corinthians 1:5). But for some of them, knowledge distilled into pride instead of true wisdom from God. And their pride was about to lead to their destruction. Paul cautioned them to live disciplined lives and papered this warning over the billboard of their consciousness: "Let him that thinketh he standeth take heed lest he fall" (1 Corinthians 10:12).

Have you ever witnessed a woman rooster-strutting down the sidewalk in four-inch stilettoes when a hungry sidewalk crack snaps its jaws around her spiked heel? Maybe that person was you, or maybe you snickered as she tripped off her pedestal of perfection. Pride is a vulnerability, and when you think you've got this Jesus-walk down, Satan is waiting to sink his teeth into your pretty pumps.

But you don't have to become an unwitting victim. Instead of pride, let your blossoming knowledge of Jesus stretch its unfurled petals into the full bloom of His wisdom. On earth we will never be free of temptation, and we're most vulnerable if we're unaware of our opposition.

But God (two beautiful, game-changing words) will never leave you and will strengthen your stance when temptation baits you. Paul left encouraging words for the Corinthians and for us: "There hath no temptation taken you but such as is common to man: but God is faithful, who will not suffer you to be tempted above that ye are able; but will with the temptation also make a way to escape, that ye may be able to bear it" (1 Corinthians 10:13). Pray, friend. Both when you are tempted and when you feel strong. Pray. "Submit yourselves therefore to God. Resist the devil, and he will flee from you" (James 4:7). Don't resist humility through pride— you'll end up submitting to the enemy.

Father, I can do nothing in my own power. Kill my pride so I can live in You. Fill me with Your Spirit's power to resist Satan, and show me Your escape route. Amen.

God's in Charge

Thine, O LORD is the greatness, and the power, and the glory, and the victory, and the majesty: for all that is in the heaven and in the earth is thine; thine is the kingdom, O LORD, and thou art exalted as head above all.

1 CHRONICLES 29:11

A wedding planner hired a new assistant. A self-starter, at first she seemed like the perfect fit. Until she overstepped her job description.

"Erin, I'm going to have to let you go. I'm very sorry."

"But I don't understand. I've been working so hard!" she protested.

"Yes, you've been working very hard," the wedding planner said. "But not at the things I asked you to do. You've tried to do my job and made quite a mess. There's a reason for my timetable, and you scheduled the flower delivery too early without consulting me. The flowers would have been ruined by the wedding day."

Abraham's wife, Sarah, also tried to do a job that wasn't hers. God had promised Abraham that his descendants would be as countless as the stars. But Sarah's arms remained empty, and she took matters into her own hands. She sent her servant Hagar to Abraham to produce an heir. But Sarah's meddling in God's timing also had disastrous results. It stirred hostility between Sarah and Hagar that trickled down the generations. But in God's perfect timing, Isaac was born.

Have you ever stepped into a situation with the intention

of fixing it, only to have things blow up in your face? It's easy to understand Sarah's compulsion. As women we tend to be fixers, and our loved ones look to us for solutions and help. We get used to being needed. And while serving our families is an excellent calling, it's important that we don't assume God is also in need of our awesome fixer skills.

As doers, we need to examine whether we're doing something God has asked or whether we're stepping into His role. He is sovereign: "O LORD God of our fathers, art not thou God in heaven? and rulest not thou over all the kingdoms of the heathen? and in thine hand is there not power and might, so that none is able to withstand thee?" (2 Chronicles 20:6). Don't be too surprised, but God doesn't actually need our advice.

"Unto him that is able to do exceeding abundantly above all that we ask or think, according to the power that worketh in us, unto him be glory" (Ephesians 3:20–21). Seek His will in prayer before hustling into action. Your prayer, trust, and patience for Him to do His God thing may be the only activity He requires.

Almighty God, I've tried to do Your job.
Forgive me for my lack of faith. Give me patience
to allow You to work on my behalf. Amen.

Every Good Thing

Oh how great is thy goodness,
which thou hast laid up for them that fear thee.
PSALM 31:19

On graduation Sunday, a video played at the beginning of worship spotlighting the high school seniors in the church. It scrolled through snapshots of their activities, relationships, families, and mission trips. Their hopeful happiness coaxed smiles to faces in the crowd. When the congregation stood to sing, the worship leader waved behind him, where the lyrics to "Beautiful One" stared out from the screen. "You know," he said, "when I first evaluated this song to see if we should include it in our repertoire, I wasn't sure about it. *Beautiful* was not a word that I would have used to describe God. But as I watched that video, I realized that every good and beautiful thing comes from God."

Sometimes we're too busy. Sometimes we're just too focused on every negative thing we can identify about our lives. But we should be living in joy and thanksgiving because every good thing, *every* good thing, every *good* thing in our lives and in this world originates in the heart of God who loves us. "Every good gift and every perfect gift is from above, and cometh down from the Father" (James 1:17). God is the only source of good in this world.

So when the sun comes up and warms the earth in golden light, when you breathe in life and air expands your chest, when your child throws gangly arms around your neck, when soft grass

180

is under your feet and a sunset ignites the evening sky—stop for a moment. God is good. Let that reality get under your skin. Let it color your day and be the lens through which you view this moment, this day, this year, this life.

Every mom knows that compulsive desire to give good things to her children. Their bright joy and expectant hope for the delights that await them with the rising of the sun should also be ours. Jesus said that if we, an evil and self-seeking people, know how to give good things to our children, then God can surely exceed our generosity (Matthew 7:9–11).

God has a good plan for your life. He has blessings for you, and likely you're already steeped in them. Ask God to show You His goodness and replace your negativity with gratitude. If we follow His ways, He promises that "no good thing will he withhold from them that walk uprightly" (Psalm 84:11).

God, open my eyes to Your extravagant goodness. Show me the way to walk uprightly with You so that no good thing will be kept from me. Thank You for every blessing, even the ones that arrive cloaked as burdens. In Jesus' name, amen.

A Grieved God

In his love and in his pity he redeemed them;
and he bare them, and carried them all the days
of old. But they rebelled, and vexed his holy Spirit.
ISAIAH 63:9–10

A mother watches helplessly as her daughter immediately relapses after her drug rehab—again. Over and over her daughter has promised to "get clean." Over and over her daughter's driving need for a high has trumped her promises. A tear slides down the mother's cheek as she watches her young grandson playing happily with his toys in her living room, seemingly oblivious to his abandonment. Her heart clenches with a piercing ache as she grieves her daughter's poor choices and their lingering effects.

When King David committed adultery with Bathsheba and sent her husband, Uriah, to the front lines of battle to be killed, the king thought he had gotten away with his sin—until the prophet Nathan arrived bearing a story: A poor man had nothing but a young lamb that he fed from his table and raised with his children. He loved it like a little daughter. But a rich man had an important guest, and instead of supplying a lamb from his own vast flocks, he took the lamb from the poor man and butchered it.

When David heard this story, he was outraged. But then Nathan delivered his gut-wrenching plot twist. "Thou art the man," he said to the king. "Thus saith the LORD God. . .I gave thee thy master's house, and thy master's wives into thy bosom, and gave thee the house of Israel and of Judah; and if that had been too little, I would moreover have given unto thee such and such things" (2 Samuel 12:7–8). David cried out, "I have sinned against the LORD" (2 Samuel 12:13).

Our sin is always committed ultimately against God. Yes, we hurt one another, and David sinned against Bathsheba, her husband, and the entire nation of Israel, but he recognized that he had offended God. And just like the mother who grieved over the sins of the daughter whom she had carried in her womb, whose boo-boos she had kissed, God is heartbroken over our sin. It hurts Him when we commit selfish acts that are contradictory to His loving nature: "Grieve not the holy Spirit of God" (Ephesians 4:30).

Have you bought Satan's lie that your secret sins aren't hurting anyone? Friend, it's not true. Your sins pierce the heart of the Father who made you, the Father who loves you and wants you for Himself. Mourn your offenses against a holy God as David did. Repent of the grief you've caused your Father.

Father, I am so sorry for injuring You through my sin. Forgive me. But great is Your mercy and spectacular is Your love! Please restore my relationship with You. Amen.

Walk It Out

And they that are Christ's have crucified the flesh with the affections and lusts. If we live in the Spirit, let us also walk in the Spirit.
GALATIANS 5:24–25

There are a *lot* of diet plans out there—some for losing weight, some for healthy living, and some, like the tapeworm diet, that are just gross. The "rules" of healthy eating keep changing, so it's hard to decide what's "healthy" and what's not. But what if the perfect diet plan was discovered? It promises to give you energy while shedding a few pounds and good long-term health. So you study the guidelines for this diet and tell all your friends about it. You discuss the pros and cons and set up a support group for encouragement. You go and listen to people who have done it talk about their amazing results and beautiful bodies. But then you never actually follow the diet plan. Your results are going to be less than awesome.

But how often do we live our faith this way? We listen to sermons and go to Sunday school, but when it comes to putting action behind our words, we suddenly opt out. The apostle Paul wrote, "Walk in the Spirit, and ye shall not fulfil the lust of the flesh" (Galatians 5:16). When we become Christians, we share in God's divine nature through the Holy Spirit. So walking in the Spirit means living out God's nature in our daily lives. It means more than just talking about God's love for us. It means being His love to others.

The second part of this verse means that His Spirit within

us can say no to our flesh. The Holy Spirit in us gives us the supernatural power to deny our sinful nature and take up God's nature. So instead of acting as we used to before we met Jesus, we now have the ability to become more Christlike. We don't have to guess what God's nature looks like: "The fruit of the Spirit is love, joy, peace, longsuffering, gentleness, goodness, faith, meekness, temperance: against such there is no law" (Galatians 5:22–23). These traits are the calling card of the Spirit's work in your life.

Paul also told believers to "work out your own salvation" (Philippians 2:12). He wasn't telling them that their good works would earn them a place in heaven. Rather, he was saying, "Get busy doing the things that prove God's Spirit is active in your life." Produce fruit, do good, love one another—this is the evidence that we love God. Jesus said, "If ye love me, keep my commandments" (John 14:15). The proof of your love is in your actions.

God, show me how to seek first Your kingdom.
Teach me to walk in Your Spirit and ripen the
Holy Spirit's fruit in my life. Amen.

The Spirit's Love

Charity. . .beareth all things, believeth all things,
hopeth all things, endureth all things.
1 CORINTHIANS 13:4, 7

Love is a choice. And we are creatures of choice—with free will and the ability to make decisions. We can choose to be negative and critical and angry, or we can choose to respond in patience and kindness, without jealousy, pride, or rudeness, without anger or selfishness. We can choose to be hopeful and faithful and enduring—Paul says that these things are love.

Jesus didn't have to love us, but He did. He made Himself nothing for us (Philippians 2:7). He cast aside His robes of deity and descended to show us the Father's love and to teach us true love. He was born to die so that we could live. As the standard of ultimate sacrificial love, Jesus said, "Love your enemies, do good to them which hate you, bless them that curse you, and pray for them which despitefully use you. . . . And as ye would that men should do to you, do ye also to them likewise. For if ye love them which love you, what thank have ye? for sinners also love those that love them" (Luke 6:27–28, 31–32). It's possible to love the unlovely, for we were unlovely when Christ died for us (Romans 5:8).

Deciding to love others even if you don't have warm feelings toward them, even if you feel deep anger or hatred toward them, is not a manipulation. "If you claim to have feelings that you do not have, that is hypocritical. . . . But if you express an act of love for the other person's benefit or pleasure, it is simply

186

a choice."* Jesus told us to love others as we love ourselves (Mark 12:31), probably because we all know very well how to seek our own benefit.

As a marriage counselor, Gary Chapman knows well the workings of love. In his book *The Five Love Languages*, he wrote, "Without love, I may spend a lifetime in search of significance, self-worth, and security. When I experience love, it impacts all of those needs positively. I am now freed to develop my potential. I am more secure in my self-worth and can now turn my efforts outward instead of being obsessed with my own needs. True love always liberates."† You are the beloved of Jesus. He fills your love tank so you are free to turn your attention outward from your own needs to meet the needs of others.

Is the Spirit's love at work through you?

*God, help me to act, through choice,
outside of my feelings and show love. Amen.*

---

*Gary Chapman, *The Five Love Languages* (Chicago: Northfield, 2004), 170.
†Ibid., 154.

The Spirit's Joy

*I bring you good tidings of great joy,
which shall be to all people.*

LUKE 2:10

Joy! What a needed quality! Joyful people are attractive, and this broken and desperate world needs more believers who live by the Spirit's joy (Galatians 5:22–23). The Greek word for *joy* is *chara*. It means "joy, rejoicing, happiness, gladness."* The Bible gives several reasons for believers to rejoice.

After Jesus sent out the seventy-two disciples, they came back joyful: "Lord, even the devils are subject unto us through thy name." And Jesus told them not to rejoice because evil spirits were obeying them, "but rather rejoice, because your names are written in heaven" (Luke 10:17, 20). David said in Psalm 51:12, "Restore unto me the joy of thy salvation." We have been saved from the second death, eternal separation from God, and snatched back from the edge of the lake of fire! If we could truly grasp the great gift of grace that God has given us—that our names are etched in heaven in the Lamb's book of life—we would celebrate forever.

Beth Moore, in her study *Living beyond Yourself*, wrote that another source of *chara* is "the joy of discovery. . . . *Chara* is the supernatural result which flows from the glorious discovery of our Lord and Savior in every circumstance where we wish to find Him."† Our lives are not wasted. We have purpose in God's plan. And He has purpose in our circumstances—both our hardships and our happiness (Romans 8:28). "The kingdom of heaven is like unto treasure hid in a field; the which when a man hath found, he hideth, and for joy thereof goeth and selleth all that he hath, and buyeth that field" (Matthew 13:44). God's kingdom is a hidden treasure—it's so valuable that when we discover it, in our excitement we sell out for Jesus.

But have you ever felt like the needle on your joy tank was hovering above *E*? Jesus has a solution for restoring you to overflowing joy: "As the Father hath loved me, so have I loved you: continue ye in my love. If ye keep my commandments, ye shall abide in my love; even as I have kept my Father's commandments, and abide in his love. These things have I spoken unto you, that my joy might remain in you, and that your joy might be full" (John 15:9–11). Our obedience to His Word leads to abiding—"to stay, remain, live, dwell"—in His love. And abiding leads to joy!

Lord Jesus, let my joy at Your salvation overflow onto others. May it draw them to You. Amen.

---

*Spiros Zodhiates, *Hebrew-Greek Keyword Study Bible* (Chattanooga, TN: AMG, 1996), 2124.
†Beth Moore, *Living beyond Yourself: Exploring the Fruit of the Spirit* (Nashville: LifeWay, 1998), 79.

The Spirit's Peace

Peace I leave with you, my peace I give unto you:
not as the world giveth, give I unto you. Let not
your heart be troubled, neither let it be afraid.
JOHN 14:27

Job's peace was stolen by calamity. He was a blameless and upright man who lost his children, his possessions, and his health. In despair he wished he'd never been born (Job 3:11). Job 3:25–26 describes his life void of peace: "For the thing which I greatly feared is come upon me, and that which I was afraid of is come unto me. I was not in safety, neither had I rest, neither was I quiet; yet trouble came." The New International Version translates verse 26 as "I have no peace, no quietness; I have no rest, but only turmoil." Only *turmoil*. The Hebrew word here means "commotion, restlessness, excitement, and anger."* It is the same word used in Job 39:24 to describe the frenzied mania of a horse in a cavalry charge. How often are our days plagued with restlessness and despair? Or a nagging sense that something is missing? Job wanted peace. And so do we.

Both Job and Peter suffered under Satan's delight at stealing their peace. Satan asked to sift Peter as wheat. The first step in sifting is to spread the wheat on a stone floor and beat it with a flail. The second step, called winnowing, is to throw the grain in the air and let the wind blow the chaff away. Satan enjoys shaking us up.

"But the fruit of the Spirit is. . .peace" (Galatians 5:22). God made a way for us to receive His peace through a baby boy:

"For unto us a child is born, unto us a son is given: and the government shall be upon his shoulder: and his name shall be called Wonderful, Counsellor, the mighty God, the everlasting Father, the Prince of Peace" (Isaiah 9:6). "But now in Christ Jesus ye who sometimes were far off are made nigh by the blood of Christ. For he is our peace" (Ephesians 2:13–14). Jesus is our peace treaty with God. And through Him we gain access to the Father. "For through him we both have access by one Spirit unto the Father" (Ephesians 2:18). Access to God—because of Christ's sacrifice we are adopted as children, given a place at the table and an inheritance, and peace. Peace that passes all understanding, peace that the world can't give us, peace that guards our hearts and minds, peace that only Christ can give (Philippians 4:7; John 14:27). And He offers it to you.

God, thank You for sending Your peace to me.
When my fears become reality, help me to
rest in the tranquility of Your peace. Amen.

*Spiros Zodhiates, *Hebrew-Greek Keyword Study Bible* (Chattanooga, TN: AMG, 1996), 1550.

The Spirit's Patience

But thou, O Lord, art a God full of compassion, and gracious,
long suffering, and plenteous in mercy and truth.
PSALM 86:15

It has been said that the prayer for patience is a dangerous one, because God will oblige you with a trying person to test your mettle.

Two Greek words can be translated as patience. *Hypomeno* means "to persevere, endure, bear up under, suffer. . . . The refusal to be defeated, beaten, conquered, or worn out."* This word describes Job's patient suffering. "Ye have heard of the patience of Job, and have seen the end of the Lord; that the Lord is very pitiful, and of tender mercy" (James 5:11). This patience is directed toward things or circumstances but isn't used to describe God.

The word that is associated with the fruit of the Spirit is *makrothymia*. It means "forbearance, longsuffering, self-restraint before proceeding to action. The quality of a person who has power to avenge himself, yet refrains from doing so."† This is a mercy-driven patience borne of understanding and compassion toward people. We can't show this kind of patience toward others on our own. It is a result of God's nature being expressed through us by the power of the Holy Spirit. I guess God knows that we can't deal with trying people in our own power!

God's great patience with us, His wayward children, is inspired by His mercy. Peter wrote, "The Lord is not slack concerning his promise, as some men count slackness; but is longsuffering to us-ward, not willing that any should perish, but that all should come to repentance" (2 Peter 3:9). And "bear in mind that our Lord's patience means salvation" (2 Peter 3:15 NIV). We are saved because of God's merciful patience.

So why do we have such a hard time extending this same longsuffering compassion toward others? David's estimation of human nature rings true: "I am in a great strait: let us fall now into the hand of the LORD; for his mercies are great: and let me not fall into the hand of man" (2 Samuel 24:14). Instead of mercy, we dole out judgment as if we embody God's judicial branch. But there's danger here.

Isaiah 29:16 warns us away from assuming God's role by turning things upside down and thinking that the potter is the clay. When we judge others, we condemn ourselves also because we do all the same things. Remember that God is the only righteous judge; we're too flawed by sin to see clearly (Romans 2:1–5). Instead, allow His beautiful *makrothymia* to flow through you.

‿◦‿

God, give me acute awareness of my judgment of others. Holy Spirit, fill me with self-restraint and merciful patience equal to what You've offered me. Amen.

---

*Spiros Zodhiates, *Hebrew-Greek Keyword Study Bible* (Chattanooga, TN: AMG, 1996), 1682.
†Ibid., 1648.

The Spirit's Kindness

*Let not the wise man glory in his wisdom, neither let the
mighty man glory in his might, let not the rich man glory
in his riches: but let him that glorieth glory in this, that he
understandeth and knoweth me, that I am the LORD which
exercise lovingkindness, judgment, and righteousness,
in the earth: for in these things I delight.*
JEREMIAH 9:23–24

The Greek word translated as *kindness* "demonstrates softness
and tenderness. . . . It is the grace which pervades the whole
nature, mellowing all which would have been harsh and aus-
tere. . . . The word is descriptive of one's disposition and does
not necessarily entail acts of goodness. . . . It is the opposite of
severity or cutting something short and quickly."*

In a photograph, Mother Teresa cradles a newborn in her
arms. Her large hand cups its back supportively, and the infant's
tiny fingers clutch her veil. She pillows the baby's head against
her shoulder, and a soft smile stacks wrinkles along her weath-
ered cheek. You can almost hear her gentle whisper: "Shhh.
I'm here. It's okay." Mother Teresa embodied tenderhearted
nurturing in the harsh dearth of poverty.

Do you know God as a kind and nurturing parent? You
probably know much about His judgment, but have you experienced His kindness?

Abraham sent Hagar and her son, Ishmael, away after Isaac
was weaned. He gave them water and food, and they wandered
in the desert. I can't imagine how this mother's heart broke

when their water ran out and she thought her child was dying. Every mother's worst fear. She couldn't bear to watch him die, so she laid him under a bush and sat down nearby and sobbed.

But God knows well both the pain and joy of fatherhood. And perhaps He was moved by the knowledge that His "beloved Son, in whom [He is] well pleased" (Matthew 3:17) would one day die. And He responded to Hagar's ragged pain and loss with tender compassion because He heard the cries of her son. "Fear not. . . Arise, lift up the lad, and hold him in thine hand; for I will make him a great nation" (Genesis 21:17–18). And He opened Hagar's eyes and showed her a well to save her son's life.

If you are hurting, God understands, for He, too, has known a parent's pain. Experience His kindness. Ask Him to open your eyes to His well of living water, and be refreshed.

Heavenly Father, You know the agony of loving deeply. And You respond to us gently in tender concern. Show me women and mothers around me who need encouragement, and fill me with Your Spirit's kindness for them. Amen.

---

*Spiros Zodhiates, *Hebrew-Greek Keyword Study Bible* (Chattanooga, TN: AMG, 1996), 1570, 1687.

The Spirit's Goodness

For we are his workmanship, created in
Christ Jesus unto good works, which God hath
before ordained that we should walk in them.
EPHESIANS 2:10

"The fruit of the Spirit is love, joy, peace, patience, kindness, goodness. . ." (Galatians 5:22). Like the other fruits, the goodness of our loving Father is a divine quality, impossible for believers without the help of the Holy Spirit. The Greek word for goodness is *agathōsunē*. It means "good, beneficial, active kindness."* Goodness has more activity than the mellow character of kindness. "It is character energized, expressing itself in. . .benevolence, active good."† So while kindness is a soft and tender disposition, goodness is the activity of doing good works.

In Ephesians 2:1–10, Paul explains well both kindness and goodness. Before Christ we were "children of wrath." Now that Jesus has come, we receive "the exceeding riches of [God's] grace in his kindness toward us through Christ Jesus." Because of God's kind heart, Jesus paid the debt of our sin.

But accepting God's kindness of salvation isn't the end. There is more to life in His kingdom. "For we are his workmanship, created in Christ Jesus unto good works, which God hath before ordained that we should walk in them" (Ephesians 2:10). Not only are we to have an attitude of kindness, but we are to be energized into doing acts of goodness. Don't get confused, though. Your works will not save you; only God saves: "For by grace are ye saved through faith; and that not of yourselves: it is the gift of God: not of works, lest any man should boast" (Ephesians 2:8–9).

God has assignments for each of us while we're here. Whether we do a little good or a lot depends on our obedience to Him. Some jobs are pleasant and some are not, but every task He gives you will be for His kingdom's gain. When you see Jesus face-to-face, don't you want to know you worked hard for the good of the kingdom and hear, "Well done, thou good and faithful servant: thou hast been faithful over a few things, I will make thee ruler over many things: enter thou into the joy of thy lord" (Matthew 25:21)? The reward of our dedication to goodness is twofold: commendation and greater responsibility.

Lord, open my eyes to the work You have already planned for me. Energize me to work out my salvation in goodness. Holy Spirit, I want more of Your goodness. Fill me with the desire to work faithfully for You. In Jesus' powerful name, amen.

*Spiros Zodhiates, *Hebrew-Greek Keyword Study Bible* (Chattanooga, TN: AMG, 1996), 1687, 1570.
†Spiros Zodhiates et al., eds., *The Complete Word Study Dictionary: New Testament* (Chattanooga, TN: AMG, 1992), 63.

The Spirit's Faithfulness

O Lord, thou art my God; I will exalt thee,
I will praise thy name; for thou hast done wonderful
things; thy counsels of old are faithfulness and truth.
ISAIAH 25:1

How do we have more faith? How do we get from worrying and doubting to "I trust You, God, no matter what"? The answer is to bask in God's unwavering faithfulness to us. Because God is infinite, without border or limit, His faithfulness is also limitless. We can never fall off the edge of it or reach its end. He is faithful always!

The Greek word for faithfulness means "firm persuasion, conviction, belief in the truth, reality."* In short, faithfulness is believing in the reality of a sovereign God and believing what He says. Are we persuaded that God is trustworthy and real?

Scripture assures us that "God is not a man, that he should lie; neither the son of man, that he should repent: hath he said, and shall he not do it? or hath he spoken, and shall he not make it good?" (Numbers 23:19). He doesn't have any of our human hang-ups to discredit His believability. Shortly before his death, Moses told the Israelites that God "is the Rock, his work is perfect: for all his ways are judgment: a God of truth and without iniquity, just and right is he" (Deuteronomy 32:4). God is a promise keeper who doesn't lie, change His mind, or make promises He can't keep, and His truth lasts forever (Psalm 33:4; 117:2).

The "Hall of Faith" in Hebrews 11 extols God's faithful servants—among them Abel, Enoch, Noah, Abraham, Isaac, Jacob, Joseph, Moses, Gideon, Samson, David, and Samuel. "But without faith it is impossible to please him: for he that cometh to God must believe that he is, and that he is a rewarder of them that diligently seek him" (Hebrews 11:6). These people believed God over what they could see (Hebrews 11:1).

"For I am the LORD, I change not" (Malachi 3:6). We might not understand why one child dies while another is healed, but we can trust in God's unchanging character of love, goodness, and faithfulness. We can't see the fullness of His plan, but we know that His plan is good because His heart is good. As God reveals Himself to us more, we begin to interpret His actions more clearly.

Because He is faithful, fight the good fight and keep the faith to win the crown of righteousness (2 Timothy 4:7–8).

God, You are the same forever. You are enduring truth. Fill me with Your abundant faithfulness so I can finish strong. In the name of Jesus, amen.

---

*Spiros Zodhiates, *Hebrew-Greek Keyword Study Bible* (Chattanooga, TN: AMG, 1996), 1662.

The Spirit's Gentleness

As for me, behold, I am in your hand:
do with me as seemeth good and meet unto you.
JEREMIAH 26:14

The Greek word for gentleness is *praotēs*. Its nuance is best understood in greater detail:

> *Meekness, mildness, forbearance. Primarily. . .an inward grace of the soul, calmness toward God in particular. It is the acceptance of God's dealings with us considering them as good in that they enhance the closeness of our relationship with Him. However, praotēs encompasses expressing wrath toward the sin of man. . . . This meekness does not blame God for the persecutions and evil doings of men. It is not the result of weakness. . . . That virtue that stands between two extremes, incontrollable and unjustified anger, and not becoming angry at all no matter what takes place around you.**

Gentleness is a life surrendered to God's power—a laying down of arms against God.

A green-broke horse will accept a saddle but has not fully submitted to the rider's will. It will throw its head and clench the bit in its teeth to escape the reins, back up when commanded to go forward, and resist the rider's direction, if not fully, at least in part.

But *praotēs* is running full-out together, horse and rider in perfect synchronization of desire, merging as one. And in case you got the wrong idea, you're the horse in this scenario. Gentleness begins with your total submission to God.

Following Jesus' example, the apostles believed that suffering for God's will was better than living comfortably in the world. Jesus told Paul that He would "shew him how great things he must suffer for my name's sake" (Acts 9:16). And Paul later wrote, "But what things were gain to me, those I counted loss for Christ. . .for whom I have suffered the loss of all things, and do count them but dung, that I may win Christ. . .that I may know him, and the power of his resurrection, and the fellowship of his sufferings, being made conformable unto his death" (Philippians 3:7–8, 10). *Foxe's Book of Martyrs* records that "after his great travail and unspeakable labours in promoting the Gospel," Paul was beheaded by Nero.† He submitted to his fellowship of suffering with the attitude of gentleness: "to live is Christ, and to die is gain" (Philippians 1:21).

Friend, what is it to gain the world if you lose your soul? Submit at last; God is faithful.

Lord, show me areas in my life that I haven't submitted to You. Give me Your Spirit's power to surrender. Amen.

---

*Spiros Zodhiates et al., eds., *Complete Word Study Dictionary: New Testament* (Chattanooga, TN: AMG, 1992), 1208.

†John Foxe, *Foxe's Book of Martyrs* (Grand Rapids: Baker, 1995), 13.

The Spirit's Self-Control

*He that hath no rule over his own spirit is like
a city that is broken down, and without walls.*
PROVERBS 25:28

Excess—we don't have to look far to find it in our society. Obesity, substance abuse, power struggles, overspending, extramarital affairs: we're being overrun by our desires and taken captive by sin—believers as well as unbelievers. So how can we learn to walk by the Spirit's self-control?

The Greek word for *self-control* means "continence, temperance, self-control."* It means "restraining passions and appetites."† And its opposite is excess and self-indulgence. Proverbs 25:28 says, "He that hath no rule over his own spirit is like a city that is broken down, and without walls." In ancient times a city's walls were vital for protection. Without fortification it was vulnerable to the enemy, who would overrun the city and enslave the people. This verse tells us that self-control is our protective wall. It allows us to choose. When we are enslaved to our desires, we no longer have the freedom to make decisions. We are like slaves in bondage, our sinful appetites forcing us into making the same bad choices over and over. Self-control guards our freedom to walk in love, joy, peace, patience, kindness, goodness, and gentleness.

Paul wrote, "All things are lawful for me, but I will not be brought under the power of any" (1 Corinthians 6:12). Satan uses any weakness he can find in our defenses, any crumbling stone in our wall. In Tolkien's *Lord of the Rings*, there is an engraving inside the band of the One Ring of power that was forged by the dark lord Sauron to gain dominion over the free peoples of Middle Earth: "One ring to bring them all and in the darkness bind them." Satan's weapon against you is temptation. And if your self-control falters, you're in danger of being bound in darkness.

Are you a prisoner already? Do you feel powerless to escape your captivity? Isaiah 58:12 says, "And they that shall be of thee shall build the old waste places: thou shalt raise up the foundations of many generations; and thou shalt be called, the repairer of the breach." Thanks to God, the crumbling ruins of your self-control can be repaired through the power of the Holy Spirit. Pray for God to show you where your self-control is lacking, and "put on the whole armour of God, that ye may be able to stand against the wiles of the devil" (Ephesians 6:11).

God, I want to end my defeat and walk freely in the fruit of Your Spirit. Help me shore up my wall of self-control. Amen.

---

*Spiros Zodhiates et al., eds., *Complete Word Study Dictionary: New Testament* (Chattanooga, TN: AMG, 1992), 499–500.

†John F. MacArthur, *The MacArthur New Testament Commentary: Galatians* (Chicago: Moody Bible Institute, 1987), 169.

Treasure in Dark Places

*I will go before thee, and make the crooked places straight:
I will break in pieces the gates of brass, and cut in sunder the
bars of iron: and I will give thee the treasures of darkness, and
hidden riches of secret places, that thou mayest know that I,
the LORD, which call thee by thy name, am the God of Israel.*

ISAIAH 45:2–3

There are dark places in this world, places we don't like to acknowledge or think about—orphaned kids starving on filthy streets; sex-trafficked girls whose very identity as people of worth has been stolen from them; lonely teens with bad attitudes dying of prosperity in affluent homes, ignored and unloved; junkies and alcoholics chained in slavery to their addictions; depressed moms, isolated and contemplating suicide. But still there's hope because God sees treasure even here. God sees, buried amid life's avalanche of grime and abuse, anger and selfishness, a rough gem. A person of worth created in His image. He loves them and wants them redeemed from their darkness. He longs to bring them into the light and give them hope and life, just as much as He wants to bring light to your dark places.

Some people writhe in public darkness. It's easy to identify a poverty-stricken neighborhood where children's bellies are bloated with hunger as a desperate situation in need of God's grace and provision, but what about your private darkness? Outwardly you may be smiles and sunshine, but do you have dark closets in your soul locked tight against intrusion—shut up tight and hidden away from the scouring light of Jesus? Pain or bitterness or addiction or depression or abuse that you've covered over with layers of polished veneer?

Beloved, the only way to heal these raw soul wounds is to unlock the door for Jesus, the Great Physician. Open up to Him, confess your secrets, and let the Light shine in. He already knows the deep reaches of your soul. He is not surprised or appalled by your musty closet space. Instead, He longs to redeem your darkness and bring treasure out of your hidden shadows.

Jesus, I have things in my life I don't talk about to anyone. I guard them carefully, and I would rather ignore them. But they're devouring my joy. I want to open up to You and share my secret pain, but I'm afraid to bring my shame to light. I'm afraid I can't face it again. Give me comfort and courage. Heal me, Jesus, so I can move forward in wholeness and hope. Show me the way to forgive and be forgiven, for true healing won't come without it. In Your precious name, Jesus, amen.

He Restores

The LORD is my shepherd; I shall not want.
He maketh me to lie down in green pastures:
he leadeth me beside the still waters.
PSALM 23:1–2

Elijah was running on fumes. He had confronted the evil king Ahab and declared a drought on the land of Israel. He challenged their false prophets to a competition on Mount Carmel and defeated 450 prophets of Baal and 400 prophets of Asherah. Then, divinely energized, he ran ahead of Ahab's chariot all the way to Jezreel, which was a distance of about sixteen miles! Ahab told his wife, Jezebel, who had been murdering God's prophets, what Elijah had done. When she threatened to kill Elijah, he was afraid and ran for his life (1 Kings 18–19).

Further depleted from his flight, Elijah went into the desert and fell into a suicidal depression: "It is enough; now, O LORD, take away my life; for I am not better than my fathers" (1 Kings 19:4). Elijah fell asleep under a broom tree, and God sent an angel to him with fresh-baked bread and a jar of water. The angel said, "Arise and eat; because the journey is too great for thee" (1 Kings 19:7). Strengthened by the Lord's provision, Elijah traveled for forty days after eating it!

Have you ever been exhausted, friend? Wrung out and at the end of your rope? Elijah had reached his breaking point and dissolved into an emotional hot mess. My kids have been here. I've been here. Maybe you have too. But be encouraged! Instead of losing patience with Elijah when he had a toddler-sized hissy fit and begged God to take his life, God gave him what he needed—refreshment and rest. "For I have satiated the weary soul, and I have replenished every sorrowful soul" (Jeremiah 31:25). The Lord is compassionate and tenderhearted toward His bone-tired and downtrodden servants. He is big enough to handle our mental breakdowns.

If you're weary in strength or emotionally beat down, wondering if you can go another day, bring your exhaustion, your anxiety, your depression, and your fear to God. Leave them by His table and partake of the Bread of Life—your joy will be restored: "Yet I will rejoice in the LORD, I will joy in the God of my salvation. The LORD God is my strength, and he will make my feet like hinds' feet, and he will make me to walk upon mine high places" (Habakkuk 3:18–19).

Father, thank You for Your compassionate and tender care of me. Thank You for restoring my strength and providing for my needs—spiritual, physical, and emotional. Show me how to deal in kindness with others when they need refreshment. Amen.

Love Hurts

He healeth the broken in heart,
and bindeth up their wounds.
PSALM 147:3

In his book *Love Does*, Bob Goff writes, "The kind of love that God created and demonstrated is a costly one because it involves sacrifice and presence. It's a love that operates more like a sign language than being spoken outright."*

Jesus shoved off into the Sea of Galilee to leave the crowds behind and presumably seek solace for His aching heart. Word had reached Him that His cousin had been executed. At the request of a dancing girl, the head of John the Baptist—the prophet who leaped in his mother's womb at the presence of the unborn Christ, whose voice called in the desert to prepare hearts for the coming of the Messiah, who lowered Jesus into the Jordan River's waters of baptism—lay on a platter in King Herod's palace. And when Jesus heard about John's death, He slipped away from the people to be alone (Matthew 14:12–13). His heart was broken. He wanted a quiet place and the comfort of His Father.

But the crowds had heard about the miraculous healings. So they followed. And even though Jesus was looking to be alone with His grief, when He reached the far shore of the Sea of Galilee, He "saw a great multitude, and was moved with compassion toward them, and he healed their sick" (Matthew 14:14). The verb translated here as *compassion* suggests "strong emotion; it means 'to feel deep sympathy.'. . . It is related to the noun *splanchna*, 'inner parts of the body,' which were considered the seat of the emotions."[†] So Jesus felt their pain in His gut. And compelled by love, He put aside His own needs to minister to them (Luke 9:11).

The book of Mark gives more insight into Jesus' love for this suffering mob: He "was moved with compassion toward them, because they were as sheep not having a shepherd" (6:34). They were lost and unprotected with no one to lead them to green pastures and still waters. And Jesus could not leave them shepherdless.

Mother Teresa wrote, "It hurt Jesus to love us. . . . Love has to be built on sacrifice, and we must be able to give until it hurts."[‡] She carried the diseased and starving from the streets of Calcutta, washed their filth, and gave them dignity and bread. She truly lived Christ's charge to "love one another; as I have loved you" (John 13:34).

Father, help me to put off self and feel the pain of others so deeply that I am moved to action. Amen.

*Bob Goff, *Love Does: Discover a Secretly Incredible Life in an Ordinary World* (Nashville: Thomas Nelson, 2012), 9.
†John F. Walvoord and Roy B. Zuck, eds., *The Bible Knowledge Commentary: New Testament* (Colorado Springs: Victor, 2004), 41, 222.
‡Mother Teresa, *Where There Is Love, There Is God,* ed. Brian Kolodiejchuk (New York: Doubleday Religion, 2010), 162, 203.

Tender Shepherd

When he saw the multitudes, he was moved with compassion on them, because they fainted, and were scattered abroad, as sheep having no shepherd.
MATTHEW 9:36

A shepherd tends to his flock. He protects them. He leads them to the best pasture to eat, and to clean, flowing water to relieve their thirst. A shepherd has great patience because sheep aren't too bright. They wander aimlessly and might walk right into a lion's mouth without the vigilant care of the shepherd.

And the Lord is also a shepherd—ours. "I am the good shepherd: the good shepherd giveth his life for the sheep" (John 10:11). And we are the witless flock that He died for: "The LORD he is God: it is he that hath made us, and not we ourselves; we are his people, and the sheep of his pasture" (Psalm 100:3).

Isaiah prophesied to the Israelites the bad news about their captivity in Babylon and then offered them God's promises of care and comfort. "He shall feed his flock like a shepherd: he shall gather the lambs with his arm, and carry them in his bosom, and shall gently lead those that are with young" (Isaiah 40:11).

You may be struggling right now. You may be tired and vulnerable. But Jesus shields the weak and heavy-laden in His flock. He is gentle with you in times when you need special care. He carries you close to His heart. Have you considered your shepherd's tenderness?

Isaiah goes on to paint God as our ultimate knight in shining armor: "It is he that sitteth upon the circle of the earth, and the inhabitants thereof are as grasshoppers. . .that bringeth the princes to nothing. . . . To whom then will ye liken me, or shall I be equal? saith the Holy One. . . . The everlasting God, the LORD, the Creator of the ends of the earth, fainteth not, neither is weary? there is no searching of his understanding. He giveth power to the faint; and to them that have no might he increaseth strength" (Isaiah 40:22–23, 25, 28–29). The almighty living God, ruler of the universe, lends His strength to the weak and struggling. This is the Shepherd who cares for you.

When our strength wanes in the fading light of another day, sometimes we want to complain a little to God. *Look at this mess, God. Where is my help? I'm tired.* But rest assured, my friend. He sees you. "Why sayest thou. . .My way is hid from the LORD?" (Isaiah 40:27). He will always see you and your struggle. Become His lamb, and He will be your tender and good Shepherd.

Jesus, You are good. You are strong.
I know that You love me because You
gave Your life to save mine. Amen.

Dressed in White

The marriage of the Lamb is come, and his wife hath made herself ready. . .arrayed in fine linen, clean and white: for the fine linen is the righteousness of saints.
REVELATION 19:7–8

They say the best lie contains a measure of truth. Satan has many weapons to launch at us, and psychological warfare is not beneath him. So, friends, be aware of the negative self-talk and feelings of inadequacy that swirl in your mind. *Satan* means "accuser" in Hebrew. He "accused [believers] before our God day and night" (Revelation 12:10). And he hasn't given up yet.

"Shame is a sense of failure before *the eyes of someone*"*— it's relational. And Satan throws it like a wrecking ball at our relationship with God. His hook is that we actually *are* guilty and ashamed. "You won't get away with that one," he hisses into our minds. And so we hide, just as Adam and Eve did in the garden. And the enemy rejoices over our broken relationship with our heavenly Father.

But his words prove false, because Jesus, our Great High Priest, stands at God's right hand pleading our case. "It is Christ that died, yea rather, that is risen again, who is even at the right hand of God, who also maketh intercession for us" (Romans 8:34). So when you mess up and do the wrong thing, when you're guilty and ashamed of your actions, don't run away. "For we have not an high priest which cannot be touched with the feeling of our infirmities; but was in all points tempted like as we are, yet without sin. Let us therefore come boldly unto the

212

throne of grace, that we may obtain mercy, and find grace to help in time of need" (Hebrews 4:15–16).

God clothed Adam and Eve with the skins of the first sacrifice. And He covers the nakedness of our shame with the righteousness of Christ, the final sacrifice. Because Jesus took our place and died for our sins, we are dressed in white, gowned in the radiance of His righteousness as His bride: "He that overcometh, the same shall be clothed in white raiment. . .I will confess his name before my Father" (Revelation 3:5).

In his hatred for God, Satan would have us waste Christ's precious blood. Shut him down when he says that your sin is too big to be engulfed by God's grace. "There is therefore now no condemnation to them which are in Christ Jesus, who walk not after the flesh, but after the Spirit" (Romans 8:1).

Jesus, my champion, I'm so grateful that You give me access to God's throne of grace and mercy. Because of You, I now wear white. Amen.

*Dr. David Powlison and Julie Lowe, "What Is the Difference between Guilt and Shame?," interview by Andrew Ray, *CCEF*, podcast, January 18, 2012, https://www.ccef.org/resources/podcast/what-difference-between-guilt-and-shame.

Foolish

*He is proud, knowing nothing, but doting about
questions and strifes of words, whereof cometh
envy, strife, railings, evil surmisings.*
1 Timothy 6:4

You cringe as the slam of the back door echoes through your kitchen. In hindsight you realize that argument was petty and unnecessary. And now your tongue has spewed anger and resentment into your marriage that spiraled into accusations born of your own insecurity. You agonize over words you wish you could erase, but like toothpaste squeezed from the tube, you can't unsay what's been said. *But why, why, why, can't I just let it go? Why do I always need the last word? Why do I always have to be right?*

Why is it that we can trip over our pride a thousand times, like a piece of furniture in the dark that we stub our toes and smack our shins on over and over, but never bother to remove it—or even acknowledge that it's there? Paul warned believers, "Don't have anything to do with foolish and stupid arguments, because you know they produce quarrels. And the Lord's servant must not be quarrelsome but must be kind to everyone, able to teach, not resentful. Opponents must be gently instructed" (2 Timothy 2:23–25 NIV).

We've all been involved in senseless disputes and wondered afterward why we let ourselves get so worked up over something silly. Maybe you need to lay down your right to defend your opinion in every matter with your husband, friends, or family.

Or maybe you need to recognize that different ways of doing things aren't necessarily wrong. The next time you're tempted to throw your two pennies' worth into an argument, ask yourself if the thing you're quibbling over has any eternal value. If not, you might consider laying aside your pride—even if you *know* you're right—and practicing the art of peacemaking.

Jesus said, "Blessed are the peacemakers: for they shall be called the children of God" (Matthew 5:9). Don't allow your pride and ingrained way of doing things to blind you to the struggles, pain, or even good intentions of others. Look deeper and attempt to uncover the root of your disagreement and deal gently with others. Daughter of the Most High, if at all possible, bring peace to your relationships.

Heavenly Father, sometimes my pride gets the best of me and I want to defend my position no matter what damage I inflict on the other person. I don't know why I often think that my way is the only way. Please teach me humility and how to avoid senseless arguments that cause division. Create in me the heart of a peacemaker. Amen.

Take Me Higher

*Now I know in part; but then shall
I know even as also I am known.*
1 Corinthians 13:12

A chicken farmer identified a struggling bird and attempted to carry her closer to the feed trough. A mighty struggle of squawking and flapping feathers ensued. After a fierce battle of wills, the farmer plopped the chicken by the trough where it eagerly dug in.

How like us! We are born naturally struggling against and running from God, bent on our own will. It seems that from the moment we can utter our desire in words, we say, "I do it my way." Psalms says, "The wicked are estranged from the womb: they go astray as soon as they be born, speaking lies" (Psalm 58:3). And the apostle Paul wrote, "You. . .were sometime alienated and enemies in your mind by wicked works" (Colossians 1:21).

We are natural enemies of God. That fact was never shouted louder than in the roar of the crowd demanding, "Crucify Him, crucify Him!" In the crack of the whip as it ripped His flesh. The ring of the hammer as the nails pierced His skin. There can be no doubt that we harbored hostility toward God's incarnate presence in our midst.

Like the bird who couldn't see what she needed through the flock and struggled against being handled, we resist God's movement in our lives. We fight against Him because we don't fully understand His ways. Moreover, our flesh doesn't want the same things that He wants. The Holy Spirit has to birth that desire in us. And ultimately, when the bird moved to where the farmer was trying to take her, she was fed and satisfied.

With the spill of Christ's blood, God put an end to our hostility: "We were reconciled to God by the death of his Son" (Romans 5:10). But our flesh still rebels against God's plans. We don't trust that His way is the best, or we just can't lay aside our self. We don't see that if we still ourselves in His hand, God can provide for all our needs, even needs we aren't aware that we have.

We don't always understand what's going on around us. But we don't have to. He is the Creator, and we are His creations. Trust in God's good character—His goodness, mercy, justice, and love. "For my thoughts are not your thoughts, neither are your ways my ways, saith the LORD. For as the heavens are higher than the earth, so are my ways higher than your ways, and my thoughts than your thoughts" (Isaiah 55:8–9).

God, I don't always see Your plan. I can't comprehend how the ripples of my actions will expand over the ages, but I trust You. In the name of Jesus, amen.

A Heart Like His

Create in me a clean heart, O God.
PSALM 51:10

"Man after God's heart" is scrawled in Sharpie across David's heavenly Hello name tag (1 Samuel 13:14). But David wasn't a perfect man; he had his issues—adultery, murder, and unruly kids. But unlike Saul and many of Israel's future kings, David tried to rule with justice, mercy, and fairness—although his reign is but a dim reflection of the hope we have of a kingdom ruled in perfect justice through Christ. Despite his flaws, in David we find faithfulness, patience, courage, generosity, commitment, and honesty, as well as the God-seeking attitude of his heart through humility and penitence.

David's life unfolded in submission to God. God peered into his heart and saw a spark of willing obedience. And it shows in the advice he gave his son Solomon: "Only the LORD give thee wisdom and understanding, and give thee charge concerning Israel, that thou mayest keep the law of the LORD thy God. Then shalt thou prosper, if thou takest heed to fulfil the statutes and judgments which the LORD charged Moses with concerning Israel: be strong, and of good courage; dread not, nor be dismayed" (1 Chronicles 22:12–13). David encouraged his son to stick with God and learn obedience.

David grew from a young giant-slaying shepherd with mighty childlike faith into a young commander on the run from an angry king, still relying on God for his protection. Our hearts lift when he is finally crowned as the king he was anointed to be many years before. But chosen as he was, David was still a man. And it's difficult to read how one so near to God's heart staggered into the darkness of sin and its nasty consequences—adultery covered up with murder and capped off by the death of his child.

But David mourned his sins deeply. He grieved this rift in his relationship with his heavenly Father and turned back to God: "Have mercy upon me, O God. . . . For I acknowledge my transgressions: and my sin is ever before me. Against thee, thee only, have I sinned, and done this evil in thy sight" (Psalm 51:1, 3–4).

Learn from David's repentance. Instead of brushing off sin as trivial, kneel before God with a broken and penitent spirit, and He will restore to you the joy of your salvation (Psalm 51:12). You can be a woman after God's own heart.

God, forgive my sin and shower me in Your mercy. Show me
where I'm not pleasing You. I need a new heart, Lord—
a clean one that thrives on Your truth and wisdom. Amen.

Steadfast

For ye have need of patience, that, after ye have done the will of God, ye might receive the promise.
HEBREWS 10:36

Olympic athletes are so single-mindedly focused on winning gold that they willingly sacrifice time, comforts, and money—all to train for their goal. Focused on that prize, their heart is set on one thing only—and every breath and action of their day is dedicated to making it happen.

Paul told believers to strive for the prize, to fix their eyes on Jesus and run for eternal gold. But does our drive for God's work come close to the undivided dedication of these top-tier athletes? Paul bolstered the Corinthians with these words: "My beloved brethren, be ye stedfast, unmoveable, always abounding in the work of the Lord, forasmuch as ye know that your labour is not in vain in the Lord" (1 Corinthians 15:58).

Nehemiah was committed to rebuilding the walls of Jerusalem after the Babylonian exile. But Satan was busily opposing the work of God. Nehemiah was ridiculed by outsiders, mainly the governor of Samaria, Sanballat, who mocked the builders. "What do these feeble Jews? will they fortify themselves? will they sacrifice? will they make an end in a day? will they revive the stones out of the heaps of the rubbish which are burned?" (Nehemiah 4:2). But in spite of hurled insults and threats of attack, the Israelites were dedicated—they worked with one hand and carried a weapon in the other.

Frustrated in his external assault, the enemy attacked from

within the ranks of Nehemiah's workers. In the midst of raising the walls of Jerusalem in just fifty-two days, Nehemiah faced internal crisis: their own countrymen had become opportunists and were taking advantage of their poorer brothers during a famine. But Nehemiah stuck it out and led the people wisely.

Then Sanballat resorted to scare tactics and threats. He sent a letter to Nehemiah that he was going to tattle to the king that Nehemiah was planning a revolt to set himself up as king. But Nehemiah recognized their attempts to intimidate and discourage his workers and prayed for God's strength. Once the walls were completed, "when all our enemies heard thereof. . .they were much cast down in their own eyes: for they perceived that this work was wrought of our God" (Nehemiah 6:16).

Is it your driving desire to serve in God's kingdom? Paul encouraged the believers because he knew we are easily distracted by pleasures or hindered by opposition. Focus on the glory awaiting you and live by Jesus' words: "By myself I can do nothing. . .for I seek not to please myself but him who sent me" (John 5:30 NIV).

God, I want to please You with my utter dedication to serving You. Like Nehemiah, let me work diligently, upheld by Your wisdom and strength. Amen.

Step-by-Step Faith

*Now faith is the substance of things hoped for,
the evidence of things not seen.*
Hebrews 11:1

Our car's GPS is considerate; it doesn't overload us with all the turn-by-turn directions from the beginning. Instead it gives a single direction—turn right. And we don't receive the next instruction until it's time to act. If we want to get where we're going, we have to trust that our GPS is giving us true directions.

God's directions aren't always as detailed as we'd like. He doesn't overwhelm our fragile human minds with His play-by-play. The mental mess inside our heads could never deal with that. We just can't handle it. We have to trust God.

Abraham was doing life, and one day God broke into his plans and said, "Get thee out of thy country, and from thy kindred, and from thy father's house, unto a land that I will shew thee: and I will make of thee a great nation, and I will bless thee, and make thy name great; and thou shalt be a blessing: and I will bless them that bless thee, and curse him that curseth thee: and in thee shall all families of the earth be blessed" (Genesis 12:1–3). Well, okay then, God. Can I at least pack? Abraham had no idea where he was headed, but God said go, and he went. Abraham had faith, the firm persuasion that God was real and truthful. He believed God's covenant that He would channel blessing to the whole world through him. And Abraham's faithfulness ultimately resulted in God redeeming the world through his bloodline. That's a pretty big legacy.

Hebrews gives an even clearer picture of God's big plan and Abraham's faithful obedience. "By faith Abraham, when he was called to go out into a place which he should after receive for an inheritance, obeyed; and he went out, not knowing whither he went. By faith he sojourned in the land of promise, as in a strange country, dwelling in tabernacles with Isaac and Jacob, the heirs with him of the same promise: for he looked for a city which hath foundations, whose builder and maker is God" (Hebrews 11:8–10).

God is good. His plans are good. His ultimate plan for you is good, but it's also eternal. Too much to grasp all at once. So trust His step-by-step directions. The temporary struggles you endure are for kingdom gains. Christian, God is calling you out in the same way today. He's calling you to leave your comfortable life in this world to go when and where He says to go, and to look forward to your eternal inheritance. Walk like Abraham, in faith.

Father, increase my faith and my obedience.
Keep my eyes focused on knowing You
more and doing the next thing. Amen.

Judged

But the day of the Lord will come as a thief in the night;
in the which the heavens shall pass away with a great noise,
and the elements shall melt with fervent heat, the earth also
and the works that are therein shall be burned up. Seeing
then that all these things shall be dissolved, what manner
of persons ought ye to be in all holy conversation and
godliness, looking for and hasting unto the coming of the
day of God, wherein the heavens being on fire shall be
dissolved, and the elements shall melt with fervent heat?
Nevertheless we, according to his promise, look for new
heavens and a new earth, wherein dwelleth righteousness.

2 PETER 3:10–13

Judgment day is a real day; it's a sure thing (Acts 17:31). And we all—everyone who has ever been born—will stand before the judgment seat of Christ (2 Timothy 4:1). He will separate those He knows from those He does not—whose names are written in the Lamb's book of life from those who are not. But that doesn't complete His ruling. Many other things have been recorded through the ages. Revelation says, "And I saw the dead, small and great, stand before God; and the books were opened: and another book was opened, which is the book of life: and the dead were judged out of those things which were written in the books, according to their works" (20:12).

So what is contained in these books? Aside from salvation, believers are promised rewards according to how we live. "For we must all appear before the judgment seat of Christ; that every one may receive the things done in his body, according to that he hath done, whether it be good or bad" (2 Corinthians 5:10). Our actions will be tested by fire. And those deemed worthy of His kingdom will not incinerate like blowing chaff. "If any man's work abide which he hath built thereupon, he shall receive a reward. If any man's work shall be burned, he shall suffer loss: but he himself shall be saved; yet so as by fire" (1 Corinthians 3:14–15).

It's possible to escape hell's flames with nothing but your soul. Believer, don't be caught naked of rewards on the day of reckoning! Daydream about sparkling crowns in glory awaiting the faithful servants of Jesus, as you labor day after day in the kingdom of Christ. Are you ready for the books to be opened?

God, my works for You here do matter. My lifestyle, my words, my choices here—they all have weight in eternity. I can't accept Your gift of salvation and fail to let Your love change my life! Lord, make my gratitude for Your sacrifice and grace burst forth in good kingdom-building works. Amen.

Crowned

Behold, I come quickly; and my reward is with me,
to give every man according as his work shall be.
REVELATION 22:12

Charles Spurgeon wrote, "There are no crown-wearers in Heaven who were not cross-bearers here below." And Paul said to run this race for the prize (1 Corinthians 9:24). So who's up for a bit of bling in exchange for her efforts here?

The incorruptible crown is awarded to Christians who have disciplined their bodies in self-control over sin: "Every man that striveth for the mastery is temperate in all things. Now they do it to obtain a corruptible crown; but we an incorruptible" (1 Corinthians 9:25).

The crown of rejoicing is the soul-winner's crown: "For what is our hope, or joy, or crown of rejoicing? Are not even ye in the presence of our Lord Jesus Christ at his coming? For ye are our glory and joy" (1 Thessalonians 2:19–20).

And on those walking in righteousness, ready and longing for the appearing of Christ, will be bestowed the crown of righteousness: "There is laid up for me a crown of righteousness, which the Lord, the righteous judge, shall give me at that day: and not to me only, but unto all them also that love his appearing" (2 Timothy 4:8).

Leading and teaching the flock of believers by godly example will earn you a crown of glory: "Feed the flock of God. . . And when the chief Shepherd shall appear, ye shall receive a crown of glory that fadeth not away" (1 Peter 5:2, 4).

The martyr's crown, for those who die for Christ, is the crown of life: "Be thou faithful unto death, and I will give thee a crown of life" (Revelation 2:10). Stand strong against temptation, and you, too, will win this crown. "Blessed is the man that endureth temptation: for when he is tried, he shall receive the crown of life, which the Lord hath promised to them that love him" (James 1:12).

Friends, throw off sin like last season's wardrobe, and replace your glossy magazines with the study of God's Word. What desires are you longing after? When we see our lovely Savior face-to-face, we will be driven to our knees with the desire to worship Him who was once crowned with thorns but is now wreathed in glory and honor!

But what gifts could we offer, save these crowns of faithful service? "The four and twenty elders fall down before him that sat on the throne, and worship him that liveth for ever and ever, and cast their crowns before the throne, saying, Thou art worthy, O Lord" (Revelation 4:10–11). Beloved, win the prize—cast your treasure at Christ's feet.

Lord Jesus, You saved my eternal soul from the fire.
And now I offer You my everything! Amen.

Betrayed

*For it was not an enemy that reproached me; then I could
have borne it: neither was it he that hated me that did
magnify himself against me; then I would have hid myself
from him: but it was thou, a man mine equal, my guide,
and mine acquaintance. We took sweet counsel together,
and walked unto the house of God in company.*

PSALM 55:12–14

Jesus' life was worth only thirty pieces of silver to Judas. Judas
traveled with his teacher, shared meals and fellowship with his
friend, but in the end his greed conquered him, and he sold
Jesus out for four months' wages. Peter, too, denied Jesus in
soul-rattling terror. Peter was one of the three disciples closest
to Jesus, a part of His inner circle. But his friend and Lord had
been arrested, and Peter disavowed himself from Jesus' ministry
three times.

Jesus gets it. He knows exactly what it feels like to be stung
by the rejection of people He trusted, to be abandoned and
left to face death alone. He understands the hurt we feel when
someone we thought was a friend sells us out through backbiting
gossip, an affair with our husband, or jealous schemes to ruin us.

You may be tempted to disagree, to think that your Savior,
as God incarnate, wasn't touched by the backstabbing pain
inflicted through the dagger of His friends' repeated betrayals.
But Jesus was both fully God and fully man. His humanity felt
the full drive of that honed blade of betrayal into the flesh of
His human heart. His humanity means that He understands

perfectly what you're going through when someone you loved and trusted turns traitor. "For we have not an high priest which cannot be touched with the feeling of our infirmities; but was in all points tempted like as we are, yet without sin" (Hebrews 4:15).

"Yet without sin." Jesus experienced your pain in agonizing living color, friend. But He responded, through His hurt, without sin. Rest your heartbreak in His arms. Allow Him to soften your wounded heart in forgiveness. Resist the pull toward bitterness—its jaws will devour you, beloved. Come to Him who can empathize with your feelings. Allow the Great Healer to mend your brokenness.

Jesus, I'm hurting, and I want to hurt them back. The pain is tearing my heart. I thought they cared about me, and I've discovered they care only about themselves. Give me the strength to forgive. To overlook their offense. Open my eyes to their pain, Jesus. What inner torment has driven them to treat me so harshly? Show me if I have played any part in their injury, and please forgive me if I have. Amen.

Sacrifice of Time

*So teach us to number our days,
that we may apply our hearts unto wisdom.*
PSALM 90:12

In *The Screwtape Letters*, C. S. Lewis depicts Screwtape, a senior demon, who writes letters to instruct his nephew Wormwood in the ways of deceiving humans: "You must therefore zealously guard in his mind the curious assumption 'My time is my own.' Let him have the feeling that he starts each day as the lawful possessor of twenty-four hours. Let him feel as a grievous tax that portion of this property which he has to make over."*

Mary and Martha faced a familiar choice: What to do first? Jesus didn't belittle Martha's servant heart, merely her time management. Sometimes we need a little Martha, gettin' stuff done, and others we need some Mary, conversing with Jesus. Jesus' truth for Martha was "abide in me" (John 15:4). One definition for the word *abide* is "to be present." Jesus wanted Martha with Him. But she was ruled by to-dos that kept her from relationship with Jesus.

Our time belongs to God anyway. He is King over even the mighty minute. Scripture says everything exists by Him and for Him (Hebrews 2:10), including each and every tick of that second hand. But too often when our to-dos start jumping like squirrels at a rave and our marching ducks break ranks and hightail it for the hills, our response to God alarmingly resembles the white rabbit from *Alice in Wonderland*: "No time to say, 'hello, good-bye,' I'm late. I'm late. I'm late."

When you're assaulted with busyness like Martha, don't forget that God holds the deed to time. He pinned the sun in place at Joshua's request when the Israelites needed more time to triumph over their enemies: "And the sun stood still, and the moon stayed, until the people had avenged themselves upon their enemies. . . . For the LORD fought for Israel" (Joshua 10:13–14). He can tame your squirrels and multiply your time. When you need more, have you tried asking Him for it? He may not extend your daylight, but He can show you His daily priorities and give you time, focus, and energy to accomplish them.

Abiding with Jesus doesn't mean shirking your responsibilities. You can still abide when you're busy. Andrew Murray wrote that Christ has prepared an "abiding dwelling with Himself, where your whole life and every moment of it might be spent, where the work of your daily life might be done, and where all the while you might be enjoying unbroken communion with Himself."†

Today, surrender your time to Jesus.

Jesus, I give You my time.
Show me what to do with it. Amen.

---

*C. S. Lewis, *The Screwtape Letters* (New York: HarperOne), 112.
†Andrew Murray, *Abide in Christ* (New Canaan, CT: Keats, 1973), 2.

The Battlefield
of Distraction

These all died in faith, not having received the promises,
but having seen them afar off, and were persuaded
of them, and embraced them, and confessed that
they were strangers and pilgrims on the earth.

HEBREWS 11:13

"I have told you ten times to clean up this room. Why is it not done yet?" In a word, the answer to this question is often *distraction* rather than disobedience. Kids set out with the intention of obeying your direction to pick up their toys, but on the way to their room they see the cat and have to pet her soft fur. So you tell them again. And this time they get there and put away a few books but then find their favorite one and sit down—just for a minute! And the next time it might be Legos that snag their attention. They don't lack the desire to obey; they lack focus.

How often is focus missing from our spiritual walk? We have good intentions to pray for a family member's needs, but our mind strays to our to-do list or that TV show we recorded. We often have kindhearted intentions to help our friend by taking her family dinner when she's overwhelmed, but we get busy. We feel pulled to financially support a ministry that is doing great work for God's kingdom, but we overspend our budget month after month.

After pointing out all the great heroes of faith from Abraham to David, the writer of Hebrews says, "Seeing we also are compassed about with so great a cloud of witnesses, let us lay aside every weight, and the sin which doth so easily beset us, and let us run with patience the race that is set before us, looking unto Jesus the author and finisher of our faith; who for the joy that was set before him endured the cross, despising the shame, and is set down at the right hand of the throne of God. For consider him that endured such contradiction of sinners against himself, lest ye be wearied and faint in your minds. Ye have not yet resisted unto blood, striving against sin" (Hebrews 12:1–4).

Friend, take heart! Others have gone before you and been used mightily by God. You have the desire, but your focus wanders from the prize. So let's "keep the main thing the main thing." Marathoners don't carry backpacks into competition. Throw off all those distractions and sins that would keep you from finishing what you started. And if you encounter opposition from the world, remember that Jesus suffered to redeem us but focused on His future joy instead of His current pain.

What distractions are keeping you from obedience?

God, keep my eyes fixed on You so I won't be distracted from the mission You've given me. Amen.

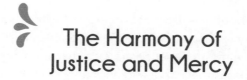

The Harmony of Justice and Mercy

Therefore will the LORD wait, that he may be gracious unto you, and therefore will he be exalted, that he may have mercy upon you: for the LORD is a God of judgment: blessed are all they that wait for him.

ISAIAH 30:18

The delicate porcelain figurine shattered against the hard tile floor. A little girl stood amid the shards with mouth agape in a perfect O, her outstretched fingers condemning her. Tears puddled in her crystal-blue eyes as they darted to her father's disappointed face. He'd warned her not to touch anything while he paid the shop owner.

"I'm so sorry, Daddy," she cried. "I know you said not to. I know it was wrong. Please forgive me, Daddy!" Her thin shoulders quaked with her sobs. Her father gently lifted her out of the broken glass and hugged her to his chest. She slid her slim arms around his neck.

"I forgive you, peanut, but someone still has to pay for this. Do you have any money?" She pushed back from him. Her wide eyes locked onto his, and she snapped her head back and forth like a metronome pendulum, sending a shiver through her curls. She had not a penny. No currency that would cover this mess. A tear escaped her eye and made a run for it down her heated cheek; she wished that she, too, could flee this store and her mistake.

Her father rubbed slow circles on her back. "What you did was wrong, little one. But I will pay this debt for you because you can't fix this problem on your own."

Consequences. Every wrong action from the beginning of time has left humanity with a burgeoning debt. But like this child, we have nothing in ourselves that could possibly bring solvency to our situation with a just and holy God. But never forget that justice isn't God's sole attribute.

Don't run from God's just nature—because mercy dwells alongside it. Yes, it means that sin has to be punished, but it also means that once paid, the debt is forever reconciled. And God Himself, in His borderless mercy, solved our sin problem by paying the demanded price with the life of His own dear Son. Jesus' death covers all our mistakes—past, present, and future. Jesus paid for you, beloved. Justice is served and God no longer sees your sin, but the righteousness of His Son instead. "He hath shewed thee, O man, what is good; and what doth the LORD require of thee, but to do justly, and to love mercy, and to walk humbly with thy God?" (Micah 6:8). Go and do likewise.

Father God, You paid the price for my shattered innocence. Teach me also to be just and merciful like You. Amen.

Living for
What Matters

*For where your treasure is,
there will your heart be also.*
MATTHEW 6:21

The headline announced THE FINANCIAL CRISIS IS DRIVING HORDES OF AMERICANS TO SUICIDE. The 2008 economic downturn triggered a growing number of financially motivated suicides across the country. It's heartbreaking to think that all their hope was placed in nothing more than wealth. Their perceived self-worth fell with the plummeting of their net worth.

Jesus encountered a rich young ruler with a similar value system. The man asked, "Good Master, what shall I do that I may inherit eternal life?" (Mark 10:17). Already he was treating God's gift as a commodity. Jesus asked why the man called Him good, because only God is good. "You know the commandments," Jesus said. The young man agreed that, yes, he had kept them all.

The rich man didn't pick up Jesus' subtle clue that God alone is good and recognize his sin and human inability to keep the law. Jesus had addressed this before: "Blessed are the poor in spirit: for theirs is the kingdom of heaven" (Matthew 5:3). God's kingdom belongs to those who see their spiritual bankruptcy before God, their complete and utter helplessness and inability to do good on their own.

Scripture says, "Then Jesus beholding him loved him, and

said unto him, One thing thou lackest: go thy way, sell whatsoever thou hast, and give to the poor, and thou shalt have treasure in heaven: and come, take up the cross, and follow me. And he was sad at that saying, and went away grieved: for he had great possessions" (Mark 10:21–22). It wasn't this man's money that was keeping him out of heaven. But his money was a stumbling block preventing him from depending on God, so Jesus' cure was to get rid of the money. Because no one can serve two masters (Matthew 6:24).

Jesus wanted the man to understand that eternal life is a gift to His followers. But the rich man was blind to his sin and thus his need for God's mercy, and the path to salvation lies through confession and repentance. So the man tragically decided to turn away because he loved his money more than he did God.

The apostle Paul said, "For to me to live is Christ, and to die is gain. But if I live in the flesh, this is the fruit of my labour" (Philippians 1:21–22). Living, for Paul, meant working for kingdom gains. And death was an even greater gain of being with Jesus.

Where do you find your meaning in life? Make sure what you're living for is worth dying over.

God, remove my stumbling blocks to total dependence on You. "I'd rather have Jesus than silver or gold." Amen.

Choose Joy

*Rejoice in the Lord always:
and again I say, Rejoice.*
PHILIPPIANS 4:4

Has joy deserted your spirit like a bird hightailing it to a warmer climate at the first frosty blast of fall? Have hard times, exhaustion, difficult people, or loss crowded out the abiding joy of God's Spirit? If you're not choosing joy in your circumstances, it's likely you've replaced it with a less satisfying response and settled for less than being filled with all the fullness of God (Ephesians 3:19). Watch out for the joy-sucking leeches who latch on and bleed your spirit dry: anxiety, anger and unforgiveness, exhaustion and depression, jealousy and discontent.

Satan is the thief who clings to the shadows. He would love nothing more than to slink into your dark moments and rip the joy right out of you. When the enemy chucks the grenade of anxiety at your joy, battle back with prayer and thanksgiving, and God's unimaginable peace will protect your mind (Philippians 4:4–7). And don't wave opportunity in the enemy's face through anger and unforgiveness. Listen to Elsa and "let it go!" (Ephesians 4:26; Proverbs 19:11).

Let's face it, too many women are exhausted caretakers, so be forewarned that Satan fights dirty. He's not above kicking your joy while you're down. In your tiredness, curl up near your Shepherd who leads you beside still waters and makes you lie down in green pastures (Psalm 23:1–3). Jesus said, "Come unto me, all ye that labour and are heavy laden, and I will give you rest" (Matthew 11:28). In this verse "the Lord promises *anapausis* (inner tranquility) to the weary and heavy laden who come to Him while they are engaged in necessary labor."* Notice that these verses say He *gives* rest and *makes* you lie down. The source of our rest is Him! Beloved, if you are weary of mind, body, and soul, protect your joy by asking for His rest.

Mark Twain said, "Comparison is the death of joy." And in the social media age, comparison is such a killjoy. But God made you to be you. Stop looking at your "perfect" neighbor and focus on becoming the perfect you—the you God designed you to be.

If abiding joy doesn't colonize your spirit, parasitic attitudes will flourish unchallenged. And because our joy is sourced from the Holy Spirit (Galatians 5:22), we can pull from His supernatural joy. We can't control circumstances or people around us, but we can choose our attitude—we can choose joy!

Jesus, open my eyes to the negative attitudes I've allowed to sour my joy. Fill me with Your Spirit's joy. I count all other things worthless when compared with the infinite worth of knowing You. Amen.

---

*Spiros Zodhiates et al., eds., *Complete Word Study Dictionary: New Testament* (Chattanooga, TN: AMG, 1992), 156.

I Can See Clearly Now

For though we walk in the flesh, we do not war after the flesh: (for the weapons of our warfare are not carnal, but mighty through God to the pulling down of strong holds.)
2 Corinthians 10:3–4

The king of Aram was livid. A traitor had infiltrated his command. He summoned his officers and demanded to know how Israel always anticipated their troop movements. "Which one of you is on the side of the king of Israel?" One of his officers denied his accusation. "It's Elisha the prophet who is in Israel," he said. "He tells the king of Israel the very words you speak in your bedroom." The king ordered them to find Elisha. And when they discovered him in Dothan, the king sent a strong force of horses and chariots in the middle of the night to surround the city.

Elisha's servant woke early the next morning and saw the army outside the city walls. "Oh, my lord, what shall we do?" he asked Elisha. "Don't be afraid," Elisha told him. "Those who are with us are more than those who are with them." Can't you just imagine his servant's eyebrows arcing to meet his hairline? *Elisha has really lost it*, he must have been thinking.

But then the prophet prayed, "Lord, I pray thee, open his eyes, that he may see. And the Lord opened the eyes of the young man; and he saw: and, behold, the mountain was full of horses and chariots of fire round about Elisha" (2 Kings 6:17).

Are your eyes open to the workings of God around you?

Do you see the same things that He does in your surroundings and in the people you encounter? Satan and his forces oppose God's chosen, and that thought can leave you shaken up like Elisha's servant, wringing your hands and despairing over your options. But Elisha saw the truth hidden just beyond the curtain of our reality—the awesome power of the fierce warrior angels under the command of the living God.

Ask God to open your spiritual eyes so you can clearly see the attacks being launched at you by the enemy. A discouraging or critical word from a friend, a personal failure to resist temptation that tumbles you into sin, an illness, a death—Satan can attack your faith from all angles. But once you identify that your fight is not with people or circumstances, but with the enemy, you can stand firm and send him packing!

Truly, those who are with you are more than those who are with them!

Lord, give me eyes to see and ears to hear.
Show me Satan's attacks so I can stand against him,
knowing that You protect me. Amen.

Washed

Though your sins be as scarlet,
they shall be as white as snow.
ISAIAH 1:18

Maybe you think God's grace is only for small sins—that surely a holy God-King would not be willing to pardon the things *you* have done. You thought your dirty soul's silent screams for mercy had been blown away long before they reached the throne of heaven. You've cracked your Bible enough to read, "Know ye not that the unrighteous shall not inherit the kingdom of God. . .neither fornicators, nor idolaters, nor adulterers, nor effeminate, nor abusers of themselves with mankind, nor thieves, nor covetous, nor drunkards, nor revilers, nor extortioners" (1 Corinthians 6:9–10). An icy torment sheets down your spine: you fear you've gone too far. You fear you're unacceptable. Irredeemable.

John Newton, an eighteenth-century human trafficker, looked back on his early life as a slave-ship captain with horror:

> *I know of no method of getting money. . .which has a more direct tendency to efface the moral sense, to rob the heart of every gentle and humane disposition, and to harden it, like steel, against all impressions of sensibility. . . .*
>
> *They are all put in irons; in most ships, two and two together. . . . Thus they must sit, walk and lie, for many months, (sometimes for nine or ten,) without*

any mitigation or relief. . . . I have seen them sentenced to unmerciful whippings, continued till the poor creatures have not had power to groan under their misery. . . .

When the women and girls are taken on board a ship, naked, trembling, terrified. . . . Resistance, or refusal, would be utterly in vain. . . .

The slaves lie in two rows, one above the other, on each side of the ship, close to each other, like books upon a shelf. . . . Nearly one half of the slaves on board, have, sometimes, died. . . .

I believe, many things which I saw, heard and felt, upon the Coast of Africa, are so deeply engraven in my memory, that I can hardly forget.*

"And such were some of you" (1 Corinthians 6:11). The continuation of the condemning scripture above breaks hopeful against our shamed hearts. Because of Jesus, God's grace covers all. "But ye are washed, but ye are sanctified, but ye are justified in the name of the Lord Jesus, and by the Spirit of our God" (1 Corinthians 6:11). John Newton encountered this great grace, just as you can. Later he wrote, "Amazing grace, how sweet the sound, that saved a wretch like me."

Jesus, the precious blood of Your sacrifice covers all. I am redeemed! Amen.

---

*John Newton, "Thoughts upon the African Slave Trade," *Bible Study Tools*, http://www.biblestudytools.com/classics/newton-posthumous-works /thoughts-upon-the-african-slave-trade.html.

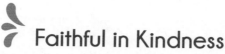

Faithful in Kindness

*"I will make an everlasting covenant with them: I will
never stop doing good to them, and I will inspire them
to fear me, so that they will never turn away from me.
I will rejoice in doing them good and will assuredly
plant them in this land with all my heart and soul."*
JEREMIAH 32:40–41 NIV

Many conquering kings sought to strengthen their throne by eliminating the family line of the former king, killing all of his descendants. But Saul's son Jonathan and David had loved each other like brothers. Many years before, Jonathan had warned David of his father's plot to kill him because "he loved him as he loved his own soul" (1 Samuel 20:17). And he'd asked David to pledge "thou shalt not cut off thy kindness from my house for ever" (1 Samuel 20:15). And because of his great love for his friend, David later extended mercy and kindness to Jonathan's son.

After his kingdom was established, David asked, "Is there yet any that is left of the house of Saul, that I may shew him kindness for Jonathan's sake?" (2 Samuel 9:1). David learned that Jonathan had a son named Mephibosheth who was crippled in both feet, so he had him brought before him. Mephibosheth must have been terrified that he would be killed, and he fell on his face before David. "I am your servant!" he said. But David calmed his fears. He'd found Jonathan's son living in Lo Debar, a place whose name literally means "without pasture," and then he restored all of Saul's land to Mephibosheth, providing him with an income, and gave him a place at the king's table: "As for Mephibosheth, said the king, he shall eat at my table, as one of the king's sons" (2 Samuel 9:11).

Mephibosheth had been brought low. The grandson of a deposed king, shamed by his grandfather's sin and subsequent suicide after learning that Jonathan had been killed in battle, Mephibosheth was a crippled man who believed himself worthless: "What is thy servant, that thou shouldest look upon such a dead dog as I am?" (2 Samuel 9:8). From disgrace to honor, enemy to family, David honored his oath to Jonathan.

Mephibosheth is a beautiful illustration of the mercy and redemption that we, too, can receive at the throne of the King of kings. When we come poor in spirit and mourning over our sins before our Lord Jesus, He is merciful. Regardless of our shame, our handicaps, our lack of worth in society's eyes, He deeds us a royal inheritance at His table as children of God.

Jesus, my King above all kings, thank You for showing mercy and kindness to me, Your flawed servant. Make me faithful to my promises and kind and gracious to those who have been my enemies. Amen.

My Stay

Thus saith the LORD, thy Redeemer, the Holy One of Israel; I am the LORD thy God which teacheth thee to profit, which leadeth thee by the way that thou shouldest go. O that thou hadst hearkened to my commandments! then had thy peace been as a river, and thy righteousness as the waves of the sea.
ISAIAH 48:17–18

Have you been doing life in your own power, seeing God as an emergency life jacket you hope you'll never need? It's nice to know He's out there, but His presence is optional for normal everyday things. You've got this. You're making it just fine sailing solo through life. Or are you? Consider the words of this old hymn. The all-powerful, living God would safely guide your ship through the turbulent sea of this world:

> *Jesus Christ, be Thou our stay,*
> *Oh, let us perish never.*
> *Cleanse us from our sins, we pray,*
> *And grant us life forever.*
> *Keep us from the Evil One;*
> *Uphold our faith most holy,*
> *Grant us to trust Thee solely*
> *With humble hearts and lowly.**

If you've passed a yacht club, you've likely seen the masts of moored sailboats stabbing the sky. A ship's mast is secured to the bow and stern by fixed lines called stays. They support the mast and keep it straight. In turn, the mast supports the sails that are used to maneuver the boat. Without the stays to keep it straight, the mast would be vulnerable to the force of the wind pushing against its sails.

Jesus is our stay. He is the only support in life that will never fail us. Without God, our lives are a little crooked and we might bend to the pressure exerted by the world and our own flesh. Are you substituting something other than God for your stay? What source of strength do you reach for at the first sign of harsh weather? This world is full of distractions and inferior materials. And if your rigging fails, you could end up lost at sea or dead in the water.

Friend, allow Jesus to support you—in both the mundane and the crisis He can hold you straight. With God's daily support, you can correct your course when your ship veers off a bit. Read His Word daily for guidance, and He will speak to you. He's present with you always, not just when your ship is sinking.

Jesus, be my stay. Be the hope that brings me joy even in dark times. Keep me sailing toward my destination— eternity in Your presence. Correct my course if I wander from Your way. In the name of Jesus, amen.

---

*Lyrics from "God the Father, Be Our Stay," author unknown, c. 1400.

Pause to Love

Above all things have fervent
charity [love] among yourselves.
1 Peter 4:8

"Mommy, watch me!" Droplets of water take flight as a petite human cannonball plunges into the pool. Pigtails in damp ringlets, she bobs to the surface, wearing pink floaties. "Did you see me? Did you see me?" Her mother smiles and claps as if she's just witnessed Olympic gold. A little boy playing alone notices the attention and rushes for the ladder. He stands poised on the deck. "Will you watch me too?" After jumping in and receiving high acclaim from a woman he's never met before, he rushes off. He returns dragging a disgruntled man by the hand. "Daddy, watch me!" But the father shakes his hand loose. "Not now, buddy. Daddy's busy."

How many times a day are you too busy to pause for a child? How many evenings are you too absorbed by a phone screen or TV to talk to your husband? How often do you send your parents' calls to voice mail? Or do they no longer call because you never answer?

Mother Teresa had this to say about our modern family life:

St. John said, "How can you say that you love God whom you do not see, when you do not love your neighbor whom you do see?" He uses a very strong word; he says, "You are a liar if you say you love God and you don't love your neighbor." I think this is

*something we must all understand, that love begins
at home. Today we see more and more that all the
suffering in the world has started from the home.
Today we have no time even to look at each other, to
talk to each other, to enjoy each other, and still less
to be what our children expect from us, what the husband expects from the wife, what the wife expects
from the husband. And so more and more we are out
of [our] homes and less and less we are in touch with
each other.**

In the beginning, Adam was alone and God said it was
"not good" (Genesis 2:18). So He created Eve and a family was
born—to bring new life and express the love of the Father. But
when we fail to love well at home, it becomes ground zero for
a world filled with pain.

You don't have to have it all together. You don't have to
be perfect. Just take time for someone else, take time to care.

*Heavenly Father, have I lied about my love for You?
Have I ignored my husband, my parents, my child
in pursuit of my own interests? Father, stop me
in my tracks. Teach me to love well. Amen.*

---

*Mother Teresa, *Where There Is Love, There Is God,* ed. Brian Kolodiejchuk
(New York: Doubleday Religion, 2010), 100.

For Such a Time

The steps of a good man are ordered by the LORD.
PSALM 37:23

Have you ever been in the right place at just the right time and felt a tingling sensation that you were destined to be there? Is it simply fortuitous that you were standing in the perfect spot to prevent a child from running in front of a car? Some say that there is no such thing as a coincidence, only small miracles in which God chooses to remain anonymous.

The Jewish people were in danger of genocide long before the Holocaust of World War II. During the time of the Persian Empire, the king's highest official, Haman, was nursing a grudge. The glowing coals of his hatred for the Jews were fanned into consuming flames of rage when Mordecai, a Jew living in the empire, refused to kneel down to him. He cunningly swayed the king to approve his plan for a Jewish massacre.

But God had already laid the groundwork to thwart Haman and protect His people. He'd positioned Esther, Mordecai's orphaned cousin whom he'd raised, as queen. And Esther's Jewish heritage remained secret.

When Mordecai learned about Haman's order to annihilate the Jews—young and old, women and children—in a single day, he mourned loudly at the king's gate. Through a messenger, Mordecai urged Esther to go before the king and beg for mercy. "Think not with thyself that thou shalt escape in the king's house, more than all the Jews. For if thou altogether holdest thy peace at this time, then shall there enlargement and deliverance arise to the Jews from another place; but thou and thy father's house shall be destroyed: and who knoweth whether thou art come to the kingdom for such a time as this?" (Esther 4:13–14).

In spite of a possible death sentence for appearing uninvited before the king, Esther went to him to plead for her people. Through Esther's obedience in spite of great personal risk, God delivered her people from Haman's murderous scheme.

You, too, are here for "such a time as this." God has uniquely chiseled your character and ability with His artist's hand to form you into the perfect tool for specific tasks in His kingdom—planned for you in advance (Ephesians 2:10).

Being called into God's service can involve risk—whether life-threatening or merely the discomfort of stepping out of the easy chair parked in the middle of your comfort zone. Get in the habit of looking for God's "coincidences" that position you for kingdom tasks. Who knows that God hasn't put you there on purpose!

God, open my eyes to Your plan. Help me to see clearly the opportunities for doing good works that are all around me. Give me courage and willingness like Esther for whatever You ask of me. Amen.

Have You Been with Jesus?

*When Moses came down from mount Sinai with
the two tables of testimony. . .Moses wist not that
the skin of his face shone while he talked with [God].*
EXODUS 34:29

Expectant mothers glow with a secret joy that's splashed all over their radiant faces. You know they have good news even before they share it with you. The new life within is made obvious by their glowing smiles and a sparkle in their eye that says they know something wonderful. When we've been with Jesus, others should notice a difference about us too. We often encourage kids to make wise choices with their friends. Dr. Steve Maraboli is a behavioral scientist and motivational speaker. In his book *Unapologetically You*, he wrote, "If you hang out with chickens, you're going to cluck and if you hang out with eagles, you're going to fly."* Who we spend time with will influence us. When people get around you, can they tell you've been with Jesus?

Peter and John were thrown in jail in Jerusalem for preaching that Jesus had risen from the dead. When they were brought before the religious leaders and the leaders "saw the boldness of Peter and John, and perceived that they were unlearned and ignorant men, they marvelled; and they took knowledge of them, that they had been with Jesus" (Acts 4:13). The sweet aroma of Jesus saturated the air around these men. In their presence, you could feel the compassionate love of Jesus and hear the courage and authority of His words.

Earlier Peter and John had healed a man who was lame from birth. He sat begging at the temple gate. He was asking only for money, but because they'd been with Jesus, they gave him something so much better: "Silver and gold have I none; but such as I have give I thee: In the name of Jesus Christ of Nazareth rise up and walk" (Acts 3:6). Peter and John could have passed by this man. After all, he sat at the temple gate every day to beg. Or they could have just given him only what he asked for. But they had compassion on him, and they had the power of an awesome God behind them.

Friend, when you spend time with Jesus He will rub off on you. His love and compassion will become yours. And the incredible might of His name will lend you boldness and courage. And everyone who encounters you will know that "this woman" has been with Jesus!

Jesus, my Friend, I pray that others will see Your influence on me and want to be introduced to You. Amen.

*Steve Maraboli, *Unapologetically You: Reflections on Life and the Human Experience* (Port Washington, NY: A Better Today, 2013).

Fight Smart

Finally, my brethren, be strong in the Lord,
and in the power of his might.
Ephesians 6:10

Are you tired of losing? Are you exhausted from struggling against impossible situations—people you can't fix, attitudes you can't change, circumstances you can't control? Have you lost your joy and hope in the desolation of your defeat time and time again?

My friend, you're tired because you're fighting against the wrong enemy in a battle that's not yours! God says, "I will fight for you. You need only to be still" (see Exodus 14:14 NIV). Don't try to fight God's battles for Him. You won't win! God is the Almighty One, the changer of hearts, the fixer of broken lives, the breaker of chains, the One who does the impossible (Ezekiel 36:26; 2 Corinthians 5:17; Galatians 5:1; Luke 1:37).

First, recognize that you're fighting the wrong battle. If you fight against people, you're fighting against *your* relationships. And Satan doesn't want your relationships with people or God to succeed. Your real battle is with the enemy—the enemy who wants to stay hidden and meddle in your life from the darkness. It's hard to fight the enemy you don't see. So let's expose Satan for the liar, thief, murderer, and accuser that he is (John 10:10; Revelation 12:10).

Remember that you can't make change happen—that's God's job. Second Chronicles 7:14 says, "If my people, which are called by my name, shall humble themselves, and pray, and seek my face, and turn from their wicked ways; then will I hear from heaven, and will forgive their sin, and will heal their land." Here lies the battle strategy for victory in this Christian life!

Humble yourself before God and admit that you need His help, pray and seek Him through the scriptures, and ruthlessly cut sin out of your life. And He will do the healing. Our action is to be "praying always" (Ephesians 6:18).

As Christians we do battle on our knees in prayer. Stand firm and be strong in the Lord. Read the Word. Pray every day. Allow His love to transform your heart from stone to flesh. Remember that we are surrounded by the armies of heaven. If our eyes could see the spiritual war around us, we would truly understand how important it is to be prepared every day. Pray! Pray! Pray! Pray for your loved ones. Pray for wisdom. Pray for God to move mountains for you. Pray for Jesus to melt your heart with His love so that everything you see is filtered through love. Pray for anything God lays on your heart. Become a mighty warrior of prayer, and see what incredible things God will do.

God, I need You! I can't do this without You. Show up strong and take charge of my impossible circumstances. Amen.

If You Liked This Book,
You'll Want to Take a Look at...

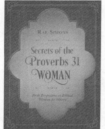

Secrets of the Proverbs 31 Woman

This devotional, offering equal parts inspiration and encouragement, will uncover the "secrets" of the Proverbs 31 woman. Each reading, tied to a theme from Proverbs 31:10–31, is rooted in biblical truth and spiritual wisdom. Women of all ages will be inspired to emulate the virtues extolled in this memorable passage of scripture.

Paperback / 978-1-63058-861-8 / $12.99

Secrets of Ruth

This devotional, offering equal parts inspiration and encouragement, will uncover the "secrets" of Ruth. Each reading, tied to a theme from the Old Testament story of Ruth, the Moabitess, is rooted in biblical truth and spiritual wisdom. Women of all ages will be inspired to emulate the example of enduring love extolled in this memorable passage of scripture.

Paperback / 978-1-63409-034-6 / $12.99